AUSCHWITZ ON THE POTOMAC

1943

Also by Eliyho Matz

WHO IS AN ISRAELI?

AUSCHWITZ ON THE POTOMAC 1943

Hillel Kook,
The Attempt to Save European Jewry,
and the Birth of the Israeli Nation

ELIYHO MATZ

Washington Books
Clearwater, FL

Copyright © 2022 by Eliyho Matz
All rights reserved.

ISBN: 979-8-8483-9770-3

**Published by Washington Books,
Clearwater, FL**
https://washington-books.com

DEDICATION

To our son, Michael Bergson Fichman Matz

אֶבֶן מָאֲסוּ הַבּוֹנִים הָיְתָה לְרֹאשׁ פִּנָּה

The stone the builders rejected has become the cornerstone.
-- PSALM 118:2

CONTENTS

	Foreword	xi
	Preface	xv
	Introduction	xvii
I	*Auschwitz on the Potomac.*	1
II	*Modern Israel: Israel as a Philosophical Problem, or Just a Puzzle?*	85
III	*The Most Important Jewish Person in the Past 2000 Years: Trying to Save the Jews, and the Israelis.*	95
IV	*Israeli Tractatus—Un Logico: "Nobody Wants to Talk About It." It's 1776 in Palestine.*	107
V	*Concurrent Resolution: A War in the American Congress, 1943. The Gentiles Try to Save Jews, the Jews Try to Prevent Their Doing So.*	119
VI	*Congressman Will Rogers, Jr., a Descendant of Native American Indians, Attempts to Save Jews.*	127
VII	*Israel, America, the Irgun Tzvai Leumi and the Altalena Fiasco.*	131

VIII	*The Zionist Movement (USA) and the Holocaust.*	141
IX	*The Holocaust State of Mind.*	173
X	*Auschwitz, Switzerland, and WWII Intelligence.*	181
XI	*Thinking Without Thinking: Intelligence in the Age of Extermination.*	201
XII	*Post-Zionism.*	211
XIII	*Israel—A Jewish State.*	215
XIV	*Who is an Israeli?*	221
XV	*Am Lo Levadad Ishkon—A Nation Does Not Dwell Alone.*	231

Epilogue 245

    There Is No Monument
        To The Native American Indian

Appendices

   A. *Letter from Dr. Stephen S. Wise*   253

   B. *Press Release from Dr. Wise*   255

   C. *News Report from PM Magazine*   256

   D. *News Report from United Press*   258

   E. *An Address by Peter H. Bergson*   261

Endnotes to Chapter Eight   277

About the Author   283

FOREWORD

I met the author of this remarkable book forty years ago, as a result of making *Who Shall Live and Who Shall Die?* -- my documentary film about Peter Bergson (the pen name of Hillel Kook) and his struggle to persuade America to stop the Nazi extermination of European Jewry during World War II. Eliyho Matz was then a young man, pursuing academic study, publishing journal articles, who had been a research assistant for Professor David Wyman, author of *The Abandonment of the Jews*, while an undergraduate student in history at the University of Massachusetts and later as a graduate student at Yeshiva University, publishing research in intellectual journals like *Midstream*. He also worked for Bergson, assisting him to define the Israeli national identity, which became the subject of Matz's earlier publication, *Who is an Israeli?*

Like Bergson, Matz found himself subject to the fate of an outsider thought too critical of the Establishment, and left academia to work in the private sector. However, he continued to research and analyze the causes and consequences of the tragic fate of European Jewry during World War II, America's failure to act decisively, and the prophetic role of Peter Bergson, Ben Hecht, Will Rogers, Jr., members and supporters of the Emergency Committee for the Rescue of the Jewish People of

Europe and its successor organization, the Hebrew Committee for National Liberation.

The results of Matz's years of research and contemplation may be found in this book. Most significantly, working as a researcher for Wyman and Bergson, Matz scoured the key historical archives related to America and what has come to be known as "The Holocaust." He kept his own copies of historical documents that are to be found reproduced in the chapters and appendices of this book -- documents providing evidence for Matz's contention that Peter Bergson's actions from 1942 through the end of 1943 "comprise the most important events in the history of Jews worldwide, as well as a very important event in American history."

Matz makes a convincing case that Bergson's activities led to the rescue of thousands of European Jews through the work of the War Refugee Board as well as the establishment of the State of Israel following the war. His interviews with Bergson give some sense of his approach to the issue of identity, which Bergson held as the key to understanding both the Nazi extermination campaign during World War II and Israeli nationalism in the aftermath.

That is to say, if Americans, American Jewish leaders, and Israelis had listened to what Peter Bergson had to say instead of fighting him -- he was subject to attacks by *The Washington Post*, FBI investigation, and attempts at deportation by the US Government, as well as continuous criticism from

American Jewish leaders -- there was an excellent chance that the Nazi extermination program could have been stopped by the Allies in 1943. Bergson's recommended policies might have saved millions more from tragic deaths, as well as establishing the new nation of Israel in a more positive demographic and political environment.

Eliyho Matz has done the world a service by bringing this documentary history together in book form, so that readers may see for themselves what was known, documented and reported about the Holocaust during the 1940's, and hopefully be able to apply his information and analysis to the thorny problems facing America, Israel and the world today.

--Laurence Jarvik, August 2022,
Clearwater, Florida

PREFACE

Two terrible things happened to Jews in the Twentieth Century: The Holocaust, and the interpretation of the Holocaust.

I first heard this assessment from Israeli journalist and intellectual Boaz Evron.

This book chronicles America's response to the news of the extermination of European Jews. On the one side was President Franklin Delano Roosevelt, who, in essence, stood mute; on the other side was Peter H. Bergson, who was vocal and outspoken. The book documents what steps Roosevelt could have taken to save European Jews, and how he chose not to; this in contrast to Bergson, who was unmatched in the tireless actions he chose in his campaign to save European Jews.

Sadly, Bergson has largely disappeared from history, as the most important institutes for the memory of the Holocaust have virtually erased him from our collective memory. Thus also erased from our collective memory is the record of how Bergson's pivotal work actually laid the path to the emergence of the Israeli nation in 1948.

For ten years, I worked as a researcher with David S. Wyman, an American historian who was my professor at the University of Massachusetts. As a result of my work with Wyman, I also worked with Peter H. Bergson for more than ten years in his office in New York City, as well as in Israel. This book is an attempt to bring Bergson back to our historical memory.

--Great Barrington, Massachusetts, August 2022

INTRODUCTION

The story I am presenting here is dedicated to our son Michael Bergson Fichman Matz, who died at an early age. His godfather was Hillel Kook, also known as Peter Bergson. This book is a testimony to the life of Hillel Kook, who passed away in 2001. In this book I explore the year 1943 vis-à-vis the American response to the Holocaust. In my attempt to examine and explain this issue, I encountered many historical questions that at one time or another will have to be answered, including the role played by the outside world during this horrific event called the Holocaust, an event that has no equal in the history of Jews.

Of course, it would be simple to say that nothing could have been done to save European Jewry once the Germans made up their mind to exterminate them, or that we had to wait until the end of the War. However, these notions are shattered by the actions presented in this story. It would have been possible to do many things to save lives, had the Jewish leadership focused their attention and efforts on finding ways to address and mitigate the horrible massacre. American Jews were not powerless. The common theory expressed by the Israeli historian Yehuda Bauer in his book titled *The Jewish Emergence from Powerlessness*, published by the University of Toronto Press (1979), is not only inaccurate, but also misleading. Thirty-six years later his student and Israeli left-wing ideological ally, Ariel Hurwitz, following in the footprints of his teacher, published a book in Hebrew in Israel (Moreshet, 2015) titled, *Jews Without Power: American Jewry During the Holocaust*, thus repeating the same nonsensical and shallow arguments first put forth by Bauer. The Jewish leadership in America, as well as in Palestine, was not categorically focused on a dedicated response to the Holocaust. However, in contrast, Hillel Kook responded in the most committed, responsible and outspoken way he could. His story is presented here to the reader for evaluation and meditation.

Many years ago when I started meditating on the subject of the Holocaust, I had no clue or preconceived notion as to where this meditation would lead me. Both my parents were Holocaust survivors, but they never really shared ideas or thoughts with me or with my brother. They spoke to other survivors in Yiddish or Russian, and I really did not understand these languages. But speaking with certain individuals while I was young, I realized that the Holocaust was not only the most horrible event in 2000 years of the history of Jews, but it gave rise to various interpretations which led most thinking people into an abyss. I never visited Yad Vashem in Jerusalem. In my opinion, this institute was created by Israelis not for the purpose of remembering, but rather to make some points which are political in nature and are scholarly absurd. Until a few years ago, at Yad Vashem there was no mention of Hillel Kook in the inventory of people who worked to save European Jews. So at one time I wrote a short article titled "Not a *Yad*, and Not a *Shem*," meaning not a hand and not a name, in order to protest this omission. The American Holocaust museum has a similar story. I never visited this facility either, and I doubt that I ever will. Both institutes offer "Advanced" courses on the Holocaust – how advanced I cannot even imagine. How can anyone teach an "advanced" course on the Holocaust? The Holocaust was and will remain a horrible event that defies scholarship. It is important to emphasize that my interest has been always to figure out how the outside world responded to this event. The response in Palestine or in America will give the reader some hint leading perhaps to some understanding. I never judged those who suffered and survived this horrible event. Both my parents were in some way fortunate, as they ran away from the front line and ended up in Central Asia. My father became "crazy" and, against my mother's wishes, joined the Russian military in order to avenge the Nazi murders of his entire family. His military career lasted a year and ended at the gates of Berlin. In the military he served as the commander of a company of sharpshooters. He never told me exactly how many people he and his unit killed, but he felt confident that he carried out his duty.

After the War, my parents moved to Israel, where I was born. So like many Israeli kids, today adults, I meditated on the Holocaust, the Israeli survival and the Israeli future. This work represents my personal evaluation and ideas surrounding the history that happened to Jews, and obviously will continue to happen as long as we continue to live and think.

CHAPTER ONE

AUSCHWITZ ON THE POTOMAC

We wouldn't have dropped it [The Committee for a Jewish Army] if it were not for the disastrous developments in Europe. We were not ready to take no for an answer.

This wasn't in our makeup. Had we listened to what "the powers" said to us we wouldn't have started anything. Whatever we did, we started knowing quite well that this was a challenge, that the opposition was going to be overwhelming. But, it had to be done because there was no other way to achieve national liberation. Besides, one never knew what the dynamics of activities might create. We had few things to encourage us. We worked from despair to despair.

(Marcia Feinstein: Interview with Samuel Merlin, Hillel Kook's Deputy, as Merlin explained the decision of the Bergson Group to put all aside in order to focus on saving the remnant of European Jewry. As quoted in Feinstein's MA Thesis

"The Irgun Campaign in the United States for a Jewish Army.")

The life stories of individuals are written for a variety of reasons. The writers love or hate their subject, according to the season or fashion. As a writer, the challenge is enormous, because so much is unknown about the individual. Writing a biography is a struggle. It does not really matter if the individual has left mountains of documents, reams of written memos, or official government papers that document his or her activities, written by himself or others -- it is difficult. My attempt here is to write a very short biography of the life of Hillel Kook, focusing mainly on his activities in 1943, and including a bit about his life before and after 1943.

In order to explain Hillel Kook's activities in 1943, it is pertinent to look at some earlier events in his life leading to this period. Like anyone else in our universe, he was born, in his specific case in 1915 in Western Russia in what we today call Latvia. He was born into a family of rabbis, some claim eighteen generations of rabbis, a fact that is difficult to verify. Then as a young child, the family left the area following a pogrom during which one of his brothers was almost killed. The family eventually ended their wanderings in Palestine, *Eretz Yisrael*, a British colony ruled under a British mandate from the 1920's, the common name used then for what we call today "Israel." Hillel grew up in Jerusalem as a child of a famous rabbinical family, his uncle the renowned A. Kook, at one time the Chief Rabbi of British Palestine and a famous Zionist theological theoretician. So it is assumed or possible that Hillel received a traditional Jewish education, a religious education, that involved Yeshiva studies, etc. And then, after the story of what I will call his childhood, suddenly, or perhaps surprisingly, this young man began going through a transformation, a rather radical one: he left the Yeshiva, registered as a student at the Hebrew University, started to study Philosophy and became radicalized. He joined the Irgun Zvai Leumi, an organization that was formed and constructed between 1931-1937 in Jerusalem.

I have purposely chosen these dates in order to demonstrate the slow process in the development and growth of the Irgun. What influenced Kook to join, how he was convinced that this was what he should do, I can only say that this aspect of his life is not so clear. To me, it appears evident that, as a young, sensitive, intelligent man, he was fully alert and awake to the events that were happening to the Jews in Palestine, events that can be described as a desert storm. It seems clear that David Raziel, who later became the Commander of the Irgun and was Hillel's childhood friend, influenced him. At the Hebrew University, Hillel became involved in defending Jews against what we call the revolt of the Palestinian Arabs against Palestinian Jews. In any case, the idea of defending Jews contributed to his becoming, in the mid-1930's, a ranking member of the Irgun.

What is important to note here is the name "Irgun Zvai Leumi" -- this was definitely a military organization of some sort, on the other hand, it was also an underground group, and, moreover, it represented the ideology of a nation: Leom (Leumi) means Nationality. So what was the leom, nationality? In those years, I would submit that the Irgun was formulating the idea of a *Hebrew* nation, the same as Italians who speak Italian, or as the English who speak English -- they speak Hebrew, so there would be a Hebrew nation. It is possible to say that the founders of the Irgun, otherwise known as the Etzel, were thinking about a Hebrew nation of Hebrew-speaking Hebrews. To me it sounds completely logical. However, I doubt that they sat down to clearly analyze the totality of the implications of their own organization's name. In any case, I do not think that they really grasped what the nationality was that they were eventually to fight for.

It is possible that some members of the Irgun did think about what is their nationality. In the year 1937, a short book was published in Palestine titled *Medinah Ivrit Pitaron Sh'elat HaYehudim*, by Ze'ev Jabotinsky. The book was originally published earlier in Poland. The title translated as *A Hebrew State*, or interchangeably translated as *A Hebrew Nation*. The Irgun leadership must have been familiar with the book. The book itself, with its complex ideas, ideas not carefully or thoughtfully analyzed, is one that Hillel never forgot for the rest of his life. It is worthwhile to note the title of this book, *The Hebrew Nation*, or *Medinah Ivrit*, because the term "Hebrew Nation" was to become the subject of an intellectual debate later on in the Zionist movement. There is one clear point here: Hillel was swept into a whirlpool, and this whirlpool would bring him into the center of the Jewish public debate of the past, the present and the future, on the subject of what kind of a nation-state the Jews want to be governed by.

A few of the challenges the Irgun was facing, among many others, were the active defense of Jews in Palestine, and the desire to bring Jewish refugees from Europe in spite of the British authorities' forbidding it. The Irgun made the decision to bring people illegally to Palestine. Here at this point one can see another turning point in Hillel's life. He left Palestine and came to Warsaw as a representative of the Irgun. He also moved around to other parts of Europe, to Paris and finally to London. From London he traveled to America. What exactly did Hillel do in Europe? -- I am not exactly sure. Officially he was sent to plan illegal immigration to Palestine and to purchase ammunition for the Irgun. What I do know is that again his life underwent a serious and traumatic change during his time working in Europe. Getting to know the European situation, the rise of Hitler, and the consequent Jewish suffering, became for him an eye-opening event. What to do with these unfolding events of European Jewry became his ongoing focus and project that would haunt him for many years. Since he was a childhood friend of David Raziel, and one of the senior officers of the Irgun, it is important to know what he was thinking in those days. Unfortunately Hillel did not like to write, and he definitely did not write a memoir. As a matter of fact, he hardly wrote any notes about his life, but upon many occasions chose instead to converse and give oral accounts, some of which are preserved in tapes at Hebrew University in Jerusalem. He spoke to many people during his lifetime. Some, I am sure, were impressed, some probably never understood him, some people tried to write about him, and despite all this he is not a person that one recognizes in Israeli or American Jewish life today.

My personal introduction to Hillel, getting to know him, started at the end of the 1970's in New York City. Meeting him was a very consequential event in my life, especially in those years. I had just completed my MA, and I was pursuing studies for a PhD, so it was a real shock to me meeting him in New York. He was very frustrated, confused, angry and utterly exhausted. We spoke for a few years on and off about history, people and the future of Israel, or what we called "Israel's ongoing changing past."

Hillel Kook arrived in America at the beginning of 1940. I imagine that it took him some time to settle down and get himself going. He connected with Samuel Merlin and other members of the Irgun who had come to the United States one year earlier than Hillel. Hillel and Merlin rented an apartment in New York City. The year 1940 was a very interesting year in America. The US was not yet involved in the European war, at least not overtly. Jabotinsky, head of the Revisionist Zionists, was in New York, and Merlin was very close to him. I. Ben-Ami was also in the US. Ben-Ami had been the first member of the Irgun to arrive, and he set up an organization called "The American Friends of Jewish Palestine." What is important to stress here is that America was a safe place for Jews. Jews, with all the difficulties they encountered in the US, thrived. Finally they had found what most called "Zee Goldeneh Medinah," or "The Golden Land." American Jews were busy; they were involved in various industries, including entertainment and anything else imaginable, not excluding the New York Underworld. When Hillel arrived in America, Jabotinsky was still alive, and the Palestinian Irgun, from many view points or aspects, was supposedly part of the Revisionist Zionists. But the truth of the matter was that the Irgun did not function as if they were part of the Revisionists: they admired Jabotinsky, but preferred to follow their own independent way of thinking, both in Palestine and in New York. Historically, one should look at the Irgun as a by-product of early Nativist life in Palestine. It is a unique phenomenon associated with a young generation of Palestinian Jews growing up under British rule. The Irgun consisted of very, very independent individuals, a group that followed its own ideas, dreams and wishes that were particular and nativist.

It is also true that the Irgun was concerned with the European situation, the terrible disaster that was evolving in Europe. As a matter of fact, they sent a team to help promote illegal immigration to Palestine, which Hillel was part of. They dealt with illegal immigration long before the Jewish Agency started to deal with that issue. This, of course, was not the only aspect the Irgun dealt with when Hillel was sent to Europe. He was probably involved in other issues, for example, acquiring ammunition for the Irgun, or recruiting people to join the Irgun. At the beginning of 1939, when the situation in Europe became intolerable, Hillel left for London, arriving shortly before Europe entered into war in September 1939. How it was possible for him to enter the United States in the early months of 1940, I have no information on that aspect of his life. I would assume that he developed certain connections in London that made it possible for him to come to America at that time. Here in America, the European problems were chasing him. What shaped Hillel's world in 1940 in America was the continuation of the European nightmare. It was also a continuation of what bothered him in Palestine when he left in 1937, and here I must guess that dealing with the illegal immigration, the human element of this situation, must have been traumatic for him. The simple reality was that, without an influx of these immigrants, the Irgun would not have been able to rid Palestine of the British. Those who were brought by the Irgun would probably be willing candidates to join the Irgun, and some eventually did. It took Hillel a while to reorient himself in the United States, and only after the death of Jabotinsky in the summer of 1940, did Hillel start to craft his activities in a different way. As I alluded to above, as far as the relationship between Jabotinsky and the Irgun is concerned, one can say that it was not exactly a perfect relationship. Jabotinsky's sudden death ultimately gave Hillel a green light to work independently, freeing him from being under Jabotinsky's shadow and influence and allowing him to seek his own way. In the years to come, Jabotinsky would always be on his mind, but

Hillel did things a bit differently than Jabotinsky probably would have done.

One of the first projects Hillel began working on seriously was his attempt to create a Jewish Army that would fight against the Germans. The idea of such an army or a brigade, fighting alongside the British, was not new. Rather, a Jewish fighting force had operated in World War I, after Jabotinsky convinced the British to engage such a brigade, and thus Jewish soldiers, along with mules, fought to help the British against the Turks. The idea for creating a Jewish army, in principle, I think was a good one, and for a variety of reasons. The European situation was becoming worse in general, and for the Jews in particular. If such an army would be formed, supported by the British or the Americans, it probably would have generated a source of pride among Jews, and perhaps at the same time would have awakened the non-Jews so that their awareness and sympathy to the terrible situation of European Jewry would be aroused. Hillel's work on this project was very sincere, being done under his alias, Peter Bergson – he had adopted this alias a year earlier, probably to protect his family name and the very prominent and prestigious rabbis in his family. His work to convince the Americans to support the creation of a Jewish Army generated some interest among Jews, and some degree of support among non-Jews. However, the official governmental responses by the British and Americans were not supportive; these governments simply rejected the idea.

As a young man, I think that Hillel started realizing and recognizing slowly, while working on this project, the possibilities and limitations of America. The political work on this Jewish Army project needed to be done in Washington, so he had to move back-and-forth between New York and Washington. In Washington, Hillel mingled and developed a good political sensibility, instincts that he did not bring from Palestine. To walk into the office of a Congressman or Senator on Capitol Hill might be a very simple thing for an American citizen; but he was not an American, but a stranger who was caught in the middle of a war as a foreigner just a bit before America became involved in that war. Practically speaking, Hillel definitely showed courage, as well as lots of *chutzpah*, to be able to do so. His initial contacts in the Congress, to his surprise, showed him that he was welcomed -- welcomed with respect and tolerance, at least in the early stages of his contacts. To go and search for support in Congress is an old American tradition. Creating a lobby was not unusual. To lobby in Congress and try to convince a Congressman or Senator to support an issue sometimes works, and probably most of the time does not; whether or not a lobbyist can win support has to do with the issue, but probably more with the quality and skill of the lobbyist. It turned out that Hillel was a very good lobbyist. Of course, the more complex question that one might ask is, who taught him what to do, who instructed him? This is a question that I cannot answer. What began as a slow and creeping process to convince lawmakers and government officials to deal with the disastrous Jewish situation in Europe gradually became a very sophisticated aspect of Hillel's manner and style. It is important to mention here his long and lasting relationship with the Irish American Congressman Andrew Sommers, from Brooklyn. If one is trying to figure out what an Irish Catholic Congressman from Brooklyn and a Jew from Palestine had in common, one can only imagine the reality in which these two individuals found a common language and understanding in their work together.

I probably could explain more of the process that evolved as Hillel, a Jew from Palestine and member of the Irgun, passed through Europe en route to America; I would assume that he went through many levels of thinking processes. Of course, without a doubt, the worsening Jewish situation in Europe never left him for a second. As a matter of fact, in his mind the status and condition of European Jewry had become intolerable, and he felt increasingly pressed upon to act. Between 1942 and 1943, Hillel tried, with the help of the American public, not necessarily always the American Jewish public, as well as Congressmen and Senators, to advertise in the American newspapers and by other means to speak about the European Jewish tragedy. For example, on December 7, 1942, the Bergson Group published a full two-page advertisement in the *NY Times* to present "A Proclamation on the Moral Rights of the Stateless and Palestinian Jews." In this ad, the group claimed the right to establish a Jewish Army to fight alongside the Allies against Hitler. These attempts by Hillel and his fellow associates, members of the Palestinian Jewish Irgun, to convince the State Department or the Department of War for the immediate need to create a Jewish Army that would fight in Europe, simply failed.

Whatever mental process was going on in Hillel's mind after failing to convince US government agencies of the urgent need to take action on behalf of European Jewry, probably taught him some very important lessons. One of them, very critical, was that in the course of trying to organize a body of participants to formulate concepts of rescue among American Jews or just Americans in general, he had to be extremely cautious and listen carefully to what people said to him. One cannot forget that Hillel's upbringing within Jewish rabbinical tradition, as well as Zionist ideology, traditions that he was a by-product of, did not fit well in America, where he was now required to apply his own critical thinking. For here in America issues concerning Jewish life and Zionism became much more complex, and he needed to ponder over them and figure out the nuances. For example, in one of the meetings for the creation of a Jewish Army, one of the participants, who happened to be Jewish, asked a question that later on would be repeatedly asked: "What are American Jews supposed to do – join the Jewish Army or join the American Army?" This simple, direct question reflected the concern of a Jewish individual who was loyal to his country, America. Hillel understood that this was a genuine concern that he should pay attention to. When referring to this attempt to create a Jewish Army, Hillel always used to say that the wagon came before the horse. General Zionist ideology always spoke about the Jewish faith, saying that it really did not matter where one came from as long as he or she was a Jew. The Zionists did not care if one was from Alaska or Argentina or Poland. But Hillel realized that America was a bit different. Unlike other countries, the United States Constitution and the American political philosophy did not prevent anyone from pursuing economic or political freedom. This was America, and still is. Here at this juncture Hillel grasped that American Jews were not exactly European Jews. Hillel's sensitivity to this political difference would later on lead him to produce a distinctive political theory that he would incorporate as a solution to the Jewish tragedy. So because of that failed attempt to bring about the creation of a Jewish Army, amid talking and thinking about loyalty and political identity, he agreed to change the name of the Jewish Army to a Jewish Army of Stateless and Palestinian Jews. This episode made Hillel a bit more sensitive and cautious in 1943 and 1944.

The hard political work done by the Bergson Group from the beginning of 1941 to the end of 1942 did not bear the fruits that the Group had expected. What is important here is that in the process itself, Hillel personally experienced a psychological and political impact. The meetings with writers, Congressmen, government officials of the Roosevelt administration, poor or rich Jews, brought upon him a dramatic personal change. Hillel was no longer the humble young man, the Irgun member from Palestine, who arrived in Washington from Palestine.

Here in Washington he became a man at the center of the world, and the Palestinian naivete was changing into Washingtonian complexity. In order to move forward and proceed with issues of saving Jews, one needed to employ complex tactics, sophisticated thoughts, maneuvering and political savvy which I think Hillel learned and acquired very quickly. So, when we see him moving on with his story, we will see that he comes to conduct himself as a well oiled political machine. It will become obvious to the reader that the most important year of his life will be and become 1943.

But before going on to explore Hillel's activities of 1943, I would like to examine another important issue: what was happening in the United States in the years 1941-1942 in the Zionist Jewish circles. These years and the one to follow, 1943, are the most interesting as well as earth-shaking in the life of American and Palestinian Jewish communities. America was not yet a participant in the War; a large part of Americans had neither desire nor will to help the Europeans. Among American Jews, the Zionist Jews were a small minority. However, there was an awakening among Jews, and this awakening would continue as the bad news arrived from Europe. In many ways, one must recognize that American Jews were alert, and slowly but surely they were opening their eyes to the challenge, to the need to do something for their co-religionists in Europe. The terrible news about the destruction of Jewish life in Europe was presented in the Jewish as well as the general newspapers. What to do about it was a completely different issue. The

American Zionist movement was beginning now to gather momentum, but the momentum was misplaced. It was not reflected in any kind of a drive to bring immigrants to Palestine. Rather, it was reflected in something altogether different: public concern for the European Jewish disaster resulted in increased donations being made to Zionist organizations. Of course, people thought and believed that with their money the American Zionist leadership might take action toward some solution. After all, America was a large country, where immigrants arrived from all over the world to live the American dream, which I prefer to call the American reality, and the American reality is for anyone dreaming for and working for a better life....Or so they thought.

Meanwhile, other events were taking place. In December 1941, the United States was attacked by Japan, and as a result Germany declared war against the US. The American political military situation changed drastically. The Zionist Jewish leadership crystalized in 1941-1942 and took on new momentum. I must remind readers again that American Jews were not like European Jews -- American Zionism was not about a mass migration of American Jews to Palestine. So one can call American Zionism a demagogical ideological movement, and not a movement that actually moved American Jews to Palestine. In May 1942, a Zionist conference convened at the Biltmore Hotel in Manhattan. One of its participants was David Ben Gurion, who arrived from Palestine. This conference at the Biltmore came out with a declaration called

"The Biltmore Declaration," in which the Zionist movement announced its future desire for Palestine to become a commonwealth -- what such a commonwealth would be, I have no clue. Thus, the convening of the Biltmore Conference, coupled with the European disaster, only brought the Zionists to concentrate not on a solution for the present crisis, but rather on one for an uncertain future. It is worthwhile to mention that the issue underlined in the Biltmore Conference is the fact that the thinking of the Zionist leadership of this period was based completely on an ideology and not on practicality, and as a result the members worked only according to ideological guidelines that did not necessarily fit any current reality. This shifting of focus to the future rather than keeping it in the present was the central failure of American Zionism during WWII. One must not forget that the direction and orders were arriving from Palestinian Zionists. In Palestine itself, there was not too much attention given to the European Jewish disaster.

When at the end of 1942 the official announcement about the Nazis' mass extermination of Jews spread in the American newspapers, Hillel awakened anew and reacted. His idea to create a Jewish Army had previously failed. Depressed but not completely defeated, he began to address with the Irgun group a new challenge: how to convince America in general to respond and find a path to save whatever was left of European Jewry. He was convinced that there must be a way to do something to get Americans involved in saving the Jews of Europe. If not America to the rescue, then who else?

Hillel Kook's actions from the end of 1942 through the end of 1943 comprise, I believe, the most important events in the history of Jews worldwide, as well as a very important episode in American history. I will attempt to unravel and document the year 1943. The year 1943 also marks a critical time in the history of humanity, because many important decisions were made in that year: one of them being the Allied invasion of Europe to defeat Nazism, another the acceleration of the atomic project, among many others. Organizing to defeat Hitler put America in a process which eventually, and perhaps unintentionally, would make America into an empire that would ultimately change the world order, for good or for bad. I will try to demonstrate some of the things Hillel accomplished in a variety of ways. What did he think when he first read in the American press about the massacre of more than three-million European Jews? Was he surprised to hear this news? The truth is that even though he had been working since the 1940's on Jewish-related issues, and specifically he worked from the end of 1941 until early 1943 to convince the Roosevelt Administration for the need to establish a Jewish Army, he was not fully alert to the magnitude of the European disaster. The official announcement of the mass exterminations of Jews that came at the end of November, 1942, caused Hillel great psychological stress. What action he decided to take likely came with no hesitation: he decided that from that moment on he, along with a small group of the Irgun, now well known in America as the Bergson Group, would focus all efforts on saving Jews.

The intellectual conclusion, as well as the practical solution, were very straightforward: from this point on, it would be the mission of the Bergson Group to work to convince the Allies about their need to save Jews. Practically speaking, Hillel had to reconnect with and employ those people with whom he had developed a relationship between 1941 and 1942. He appealed to his friend and supporter Ben Hecht, the talented writer, playwright and master of the written word. Hecht was a complex American individual who discovered his Jewishness late in his career. Early in his career, when he was a reporter in Chicago, he hardly dealt or occupied himself with Jewish issues. Further on in his career, he wrote a book in which he described the main character, a Jew, as a lowlife. Later he was to go on a win an Oscar Award for his screenplay for the movie *The Front Page*. Among his other achievements was writing the final version of the screenplay for *Gone With The Wind*. After that Hecht arrived in New York, where in the early 1940's he and Hillel met. At that time he was writing an article for one of the New York City newspapers, about the terrible situation for the Jews in Europe. Hillel seized the moment to contact Hecht, and thus a very meaningful relationship developed. Ben Hecht, full of energy, vigor and imagination, joined with Hillel's assistant Samuel Merlin to write the pageant "We Will Never Die." Hecht was well connected to the entertainment world of actors, musicians and theater producers, some of them extremely talented, and it was to many of them that he appealed for help in producing the pageant.

In preparation for this pageant, Hecht wrote an article that appeared in the *PM* newspaper on February 22, 1943, in which he emotionally expressed his feelings about America and the ongoing Holocaust, and I quote in full:

A Letter From Ben Hecht

A memorial service for the 2,000,000 massacred Jews of Europe will be conducted in Madison Square Garden on March 9. Billy Rose is in charge and a committee including Kurt Weill, Moss Hart, myself, Lemuel Ayers, Peter Bergson and innumerable Americans of every creed is involved in its production. Tickets are available at Room 701, 1 East 44th St. The appended essay is an explanation of this activity.—B.H.

The Jewish situation is becoming less and less complex. For one thing, it has no longer much to do with Jews. Their extermination is removing them from any and all situations.

As a matter of fact, the Jewish situation never has had much to do with Jews. The hating and killing of Jews has been one of the unlovely sides of history – not Jewish history, but everybody else's history. The Jews have been a lightning rod down which a thousand different psychic storms have struck and vented themselves.

This has given the Jew a bad name. His historical position as a target has inspired countless thinkers to investigate the "curious" qualities that have made him a target. Investigation of the qualities that have inspired mass murder in his enemies has been less active.

I will write about this later. I am writing about something else now.

The Jewish situation has undergone a change unique in history, for the incontrovertible reason that he is being wiped out in Europe – where he was so great a Problem.

Two millions have already been killed. There are some four millions of Jews remaining in Europe, a fact that is outrageous to the German philosophers. To remedy this blot on civilization, the Germans have announced officially that they are going to speed up their anti-Jew procedures. They are going to exterminate four million Jews by Christmas.

Death is no great novelty these days. Everybody has to die some time. Many soldiers have to die – maybe millions – in a very short time. So the killing of four million more Jews in time for the Christmas holidays apparently is nothing to inspire astonishment.

Even the manner in which this Christmas package of dead Jews is being prepared for the world – the barbarisms attending the massacre – has inspired to date a minimum of astonishment.

We live in a world in which many things have come to be taken for granted. It is taken for granted that massacre must be crueler than war. Once you have bashed in a million defenseless skulls, massacre loses its original appeal. You have to invent things to keep it exciting. It is taken for granted that the numerous diverting procedures the

Germans have injected into the killing of Jews are a natural part of massacre.

With the killing of the four million remaining Jews of Europe, Hans and Fritz will have solved to a great extent the Jewish problem in a great many places. They will, however, have created another problem of much greater proportions. This is the problem of what humanity – as the civilized peoples of the world are still called – is going to do about it.

To date, humanity has done almost nothing. Its indignation has been small. It has raised no sustained official voice. It has shuddered and taken matters for granted.

In fact, the German massacre of 2,000,000 human beings without guns or sticks with which to defend themselves has been possible only because humanity has stuck its skull into a fog. Its nerve endings are apparently dead, its ears blunted, its eyes a little crossed and out of focus. It has been running to disasters until it is out of breath and it doesn't much care whether school keeps or not.

This is the new Jewish situation – a situation independent of Jews, alive or dead.

The numbness of our American folks, small and great, is as striking an exhibition of life fallen into humanless ways as the massacre-politik of the Germans. We who have stood by silently at the overthrow of basic human reason and sensibilities have been honorary members of the German posse.

Our writers fill their columns daily with intrepid denunciations and exposures of the Tweedledum-Tweedledee political confusion in the world. They see human disaster in this scheme and that project. They fret about the future of the airways and lock heroic horns on the problems of taxation. But of this overthrow the basic concepts of life, of this plunge into the ways of savagery, of this great backward step into massacre, they speak almost not at all.

It is for this reason that we are staging a memorial service in Madison Square Garden for the dead Jews of Europe. The service will be held on the night of March 9. It is believed that Governor Dewey is setting this day aside as a day of prayer, not Jewish prayer, but American prayer, for the massacred people of Europe.

Our memorial service is an attempt to cope with the Jewish situation as it exists in the befogged and bemused soul of our town. We are not going to make speeches. We are going instead to sing a Kaddish for the two million dead. We are going to bring a Madison Square Garden audience to the large grave of Jewry and let them stand for two hours looking into its remarkable contents.

We are not going to denounce Hitler, if there is a Hitler. It is our thought that Hitler is a back number – a sort of Typhus Mary – who has had his day. He has blown his germs far and wide across seas and continents.

The germs we are combating are those of spiritual corruption that have burrowed deep into the soul of man. There aren't many Nazis in New York today. But there are a myriad of numb people with hearts deader than doornails, and there will be myriads more with every month that passes. These are the new Jewish situation.

It is for these -- Jews, Christians, Mohammedans, agnostics and Atheists -- that we are conducting our memorial service. It is to sing a song over their befogged and preoccupied heads and wake them for an hour or two to the degeneration of life taking place, that we are dedicating our efforts.

What good will it do? Will it save Jews from having their four million defenseless heads bashed in, from being burned in piles like the refuse on Riker's Island? I don't know. Maybe we can awaken some of the vacationing hearts in our government. And maybe we can induce a voice to sound somewhere in behalf of human dignity – a voice powerful enough to cause Hans and Fritz to pause and blink and drop their happy extermination torches.

But whether or not such objective is achieved, one thing we can promise: We can promise that the numbness will be lifted for two hours from all who come to our memorial service. We can promise that the song to the two million Jewish dead will not rise entirely in vain.

We have no other objective than this. No money is to be raised for any cause. No profits are to accrue for any group or organization. We are making only propaganda and our propaganda is a call to sing for the dead. They have passed the Jewish situation on to the living.

I solicit the editors of PM who have managed to keep their souls from falling asleep under the lullaby of disasters to help us invite their readers to our memorial service. And to print these tidings as our invitation to the town.

BEN HECHT

Ben Hecht tried to alert major Jewish organizations to the fact that he was working on a pageant to memorialize the murdered Jews of Europe, and, of course naively, he thought that these Jewish organizations would work together with him on this critical project. In hindsight, the response of the American Jewish Committee to this effort was disturbing and disappointing, to say the least:

Ben Hecht did two things: he presented a plan for an historical pageant which he and an unnamed group of writers and artists who would contribute their services would stage. The pageant would depict the history of the Jews, their contribution to civilization, but emphasize more than everything else a "Kadish" for the Jews who are now being slaughtered in Nazi dominated Europe and a plea or a demand for an aroused Christian conscience. His second point was that he got into this partly because of his own feelings and partly through the collaboration of the Committee for a Jewish Army.

Whereupon Bergson one of the revisionist leaders of the Committee for a Jewish

Army, spoke up and declared that although he and his group had investigated and would give it every cooperation, in the interests of harmony he would be glad to withdraw the sponsorship of his organization if that would elicit the sponsorship of a united Jewry....

I indicated for the AJC "no comment but would transmit results of the meeting"....

When the people who were leaving the meeting pressed for more positive answers from the Labor Committee, the [American Jewish] Congress and myself, Dennen and I indicated that you could not very easily and very suddenly build a united front which would involve all these organizations,...and that we personally were skeptical that it could be done....

The meeting obviously was initiated by the Committee for a Jewish Army who apparently have taken in Ben Hecht in the way they had taken in the recently resigned Pierre van Paassen. They may in fact produce a pageant and have Hecht and some of his friends do it. It may even have literary merit (his article in the current issue of the <u>American Mercury</u> is excellent.) Obviously, we as a Committee should have nothing to do with this venture.

[Frank N. Trager to David Rosenblum, Memorandum, February 1, 1943; File: Mr. Proskauer, Emergency Committee 43-44, AJ Committee Archives.]

The performance took place in Madison Square Garden in March 1943, and attracted thousands of people. Additional thousands stood outside. It was a well done, very effective production that eventually toured a number of cities around the US, among them Philadelphia, Chicago, Los Angeles and Constitution Hall in Washington, DC.

Following is a quote from a column by Eleanor Roosevelt, published in April 1943, in newspapers distributed around the United States in reference to this event at Constitution Hall:

In the evening we attended a mass memorial in Constitution Hall dedicated to the 2,000,000 Jewish dead of Europe. It was called, 'We Shall Never Die.' Flags of all the nations occupied by Germany came on the stage.

The music, singing, narration and actors all served to make it one of the most impressive and moving pageants I have ever seen. No one who heard each group come forward and give the story of what had happened to it at the hands of a ruthless German military machine, will ever forget those haunting words: "Remember Us."

All the way through, I thought how important it is in this country that we do not for a moment allow intolerance and cruelty to creep into our dealings with any of our own people or with any people who have taken refuge among us. Even with our enemies, I hope we shall always remember that cruelty is a double-edged sword, destroying not only the victim, but the person who indulges in it.

Hillel was invited twice to the White House by Mrs. Roosevelt for a conversation on the mass killing of European Jewry. His efforts to convince her to take any action, with her husband or otherwise, were not successful.

At the same time that Hillel, with the help of Ben Hecht, was trying to awaken America, what were the American Zionists doing? The American Zionists also held their own memorial service for the European Jewish victims, but the important difference was, their efforts were not so much focused on awakening America as they were on pushing their own Zionist agenda. I examined and wrote about this failure many years ago as part of my research in a document that I will include later on in this book (see Chapter Eight). The American Zionists pushed Zionist goals: one cannot forget that the Zionists had a goal, as underlined in their Biltmore Declaration in May 1942, and that goal was not how to save Jews at that moment, but rather how to deal with them only after the War -- a tragically ludicrous concept, for how could they build a State after most of its potential inhabitants had been massacred? The Zionists did not focus on rescue. Moreover, what they did was to try to disturb and inhibit the activities of the Bergson Group.

It was at this time, the Bergson Group began to move very forcefully and started a campaign of full-page advertisements in prominent American newspapers. For example, on February 8, 1943, in a *NY Times* ad, the Bergson Group demanded "Action, Not Pity" as the way to save European Jewry. Other samples of these advertisements will follow below. The purpose of these full-page advertisements was to awaken America, to create a public opinion, and basically to convince the US Government, if possible, to take action on behalf of European Jews. These full-page advertisements appealed not only to American Jews, but also to the American public at-large, and one of the results was that they brought financial contributions to the Bergson Group's organization. Otherwise it would be difficult to understand how they were able to continue to publish these ads in the American newspapers. In an article I published in *Gesher*, a student publication of Yeshiva University ("An Analysis of the Pressure Group: The Activities of the Bergson Group in the Year 1943," Vol.8, 5741/1981), I reviewed some of these advertisements.

By examining the evolution of the ads, one can trace the historical development of the attitude of the Bergson group towards rescue:

December 5, 1942 – *New York Times*: "To the Conscience of America" is the address which headed this advertisement signed by Pierre van Passen. Van Passen commenced by recounting the horror of the Nazi massacres, saying, "Men, women and children are pressed into air-tight chambers where they are choked to death en masse with poison gas...." He asked people to speak out, for the sake of humanity, against the exterminations: "America is not to have the blood-guilt of these millions on its conscience!" Van Passen inserted an appeal to Americans to exercise their power to subvert Hitler's aim.

He proposed that "...an American Commission of military and governmental experts...find a way to stop this wholesale murder!" The ad concluded with a call for the organization of a Jewish army to fight back against Hitler.

December 7, 1942 – *New York Times*: The Bergson group submitted a full two-page advertisement presenting "A Proclamation On the Moral Rights of the Stateless and Palestinian Jews." The group claimed the right to establish a Jewish Army to fight alongside the Allies against Hitler. Their concern for a Jewish Army still remained the Bergsonites' primary focus.

February 8, 1943 – *New York Times*: "Action, Not Pity" is what the Bergson group demanded as the way to save European Jewry. They recounted in this article the story of the annihilation of the Jews and proposed some measures toward halting the Nazi extermination process. Their first suggestion was for the United Nations [the "United Nations" of this period were those Allied Nations united against the Axis Countries] to "consider the cessation of atrocities against the Jews as an immediate aim of their military and political operations," and only *secondly* did they call for official approval for establishing a Jewish Army of Stateless and Palestinian Jews.

February 16, 1943 – *New York Times*: In its response to a news report published in the *New York Times* on February 12, 1943 (p. 5), which discussed the possible ransom of Rumanian Jewry, the Bergson group produced an eye-catching advertisement captioned, "For Sale to Humanity – 70,000 Jews, Guaranteed Human Beings at $50 a Piece." Bordering the left side of the ad was a column article which explained the proposal to ransom Rumanian Jews. The ad was constructed as a collage of material pertinent to this issue. To the right of the page beneath the caption was the following letter written by Ben Hecht:

To The FOUR FREEDOMS:
Care United Nations' Leaders.

My Dear Noble States of Mind:

I know you are very, very busy, too busy perhaps to read the story on the left-hand side of this page. For that reason I am writing an ad. Ads are easier and quicker to read than stories.

Your admirer,

Ben Hecht

The advertisement presented an appeal to American people to support the rescue of 70,000

Rumanian Jews by sending money to the Bergson Committee to be used to help raise the consciousness of the American people and their leaders, and to help spread the news of the new possibility for rescue.

March 10, 1943 – *New York Times*: Another full-page ad appeared with a letter by Senator Johnson. The headline read: "Save the 4,000,000 remaining Jews of Europe by Action – Not Pity!" Johnson cited the strong response to the Committee's March 9 pageant in Madison Square Garden as proof that "the conspiracy of silence" that surrounded the Jewish disaster in Europe had definitely been "broken now." He advocated three proposed measures:

1) To establish an inter-governmental commission to stop the exterminations;
2) to establish a Jewish Army;
3) to transfer Jews to Palestine.

These three demands make apparent what the priorities of the Bergson group were, and it becomes evident from this point on, through the subsequent actions and statements of the Committee, that its primary task was to work toward the creation of a governmental agency to rescue Jews.

March 15, 1943 – *New York Journal American* and *New York Post*: When

Britain's Foreign Minister, Anthony Eden, visited Washington in March 1943, the Bergson group published a full-page advertisement headlined with the plea, "Mr. Hull-Mr. Eden – Allies for Humanity, Can You Not Hear the Message of Your Peoples? Action – Not Pity, Can Save Millions Now!" The *New York Journal American* included a picture from the Madison Square Garden demonstration of March 9, 1943. The ad reiterated the primary demand for an intergovernmental commission of military experts to start work on the rescue of Jews. In this piece, the group also proposed that suicide squads be used to save Jews, and that a Jewish Army be established.

April 5, 1943 – *Washington Post*: In this advertisement, the Bergson group again restated its claim that the establishment of a United Nations Agency to rescue Jews was its primary concern. The same demand appeared in the *New York Times* on April 13, 1943. In addition, the group interjected two further motions, to transfer Jews to Palestine, and to create a Jewish Army.

May 4, 1943 – *New York Times*; **May 6, 1943** – *New York Post*: The conviction that the United Nations should establish an agency to rescue Jews and strive to halt the annihilation process blossomed to its fullest potential in an ad published after the

Bermuda Conference. The advertisement asserted, "To 5,000,000 Jews in the Nazi Death-Trap, Bermuda was a 'Cruel Mockery'." The sub-title reflected the group's top concern: "When Will the United Nations Establish An Agency To Deal With The Problem of a Whole People?"

So, a great pageant by Ben Hecht, famous American actors and full-page advertisements created a vast amount of momentum and awakened the American public to the ongoing European disaster. In addition, with the help of Samuel Merlin, Hillel created a magazine called *The Answer*, whose purpose it was to highlight the tragedy of European Jews. This magazine included articles written by prominent Americans who supported the Bergson Group in its attempt to save European Jews.

Once the public was awakened, Hillel felt that he had to seize the moment and try to convince the American Government to take some action. While talking in the halls of Congress, or visiting Government offices, he felt that he had to take some dramatic action to change the US Government's hesitant attitude toward saving Jews. On April 19, 1943, the Allies convened a conference in Bermuda, choosing this location purposely to make it inaccessible to any Jewish delegation. This Conference, organized by the American and British governments, ensured that implementing any plan to save Jews would be prevented. So in response, Hillel published a very powerful full-page advertisement in the *NY Times* and other newspapers titled, "To

5,000,000 Jews in the Nazi Death-Trap Bermuda Was a 'Cruel Mockery.'" This ad created strong verbal criticism in the Senate of the United States by one of the Senators who participated in the Conference, and Senator Harry Truman sent a nasty note to Bergson because of it. Hillel then decided to convene his own conference to deliberate over how to save European Jewry, choosing Manhattan as his location knowing that this place would be very accessible to all participants. This was exactly opposite to what the Allies attempted to manipulate in Bermuda in April. Consequently, in June 1943, Kook called for a conference to convene in Manhattan, in which various ideas on how to save European Jewry would be examined and discussed.

From July 20-25, 1943, the Emergency Conference to Save the Jewish People of Europe was held at the Hotel Commodore in Manhattan. It was Hillel's brainchild and planning that brought together dozens of experts for a serious, multifaceted conversation on the possibilities that were available for the Allies to save Jews. Congressmen, Senators, and all sorts of knowledgeable individuals familiar with war issues such as shipping and rescue were invited. Among them was Will Rogers, Jr., a Democrat Congressman from California, who not only participated, but also traveled on behalf of the Conference to England. In England, he attempted to discuss the possibilities to rescue Jews with British officials, but he failed to move them and returned empty-handed. The British were not willing to lift a finger to save Jews. Out of frustration and after deliberations, Hillel persuaded Will Rogers, Jr., and other Congressmen, of the soundness of crafting a resolution to save the Jews of Europe to be presented in the US House of Representatives. In the Senate, Hillel convinced Senators Guy Gillette and Elbert Thomas to do the same. This concurrent resolution would be sort of a call, a challenge, for a possible act of mercy from the Roosevelt Administration to take some action to save European Jews.

We need to say, or tell here, something about Franklin Delano Roosevelt, because it will help to clarify the story we are trying to tell. Roosevelt was one of the most important Presidents in the history of the United States, probably as important as Lincoln. He was a crippled individual, a son of wealthy Americans, who did his best to pull America out of a terrible economic depression that struck the US in 1929. He also led America in a world war, a war that demanded radical changes in all aspects of American life. American Jews were his early political supporters. Some of his closest aides were Jewish. The role played by the Jews who were close to Roosevelt is still an enigma today vis-à-vis the issue of saving European Jewry. And with all the superlatives I have said above, he did hardly anything to save Jews. Why he behaved the way he did leads us to lots of speculation.

At the University of Massachusetts, where I studied Jewish History and Political Science, I asked my professor, David S. Wyman, who taught Modern American History, if by any chance he had found any documents that pointed to the fact of when Roosevelt had concrete knowledge of the Holocaust. Dr. Wyman's answer was that he had searched many years for such documentation but had come up empty-handed. A few years later, while doing research for my MA in New York City, I found a document in an archive that brought us closer to the answer of when and what the President knew. Apparently he knew quite a bit.

On December 8, 1942, Roosevelt greeted a gathering of his invited guests, the entire American Jewish leadership, in the White House. There, at noontime, he told those assembled, straightforward, that the official announcement in late November 1942, about the massacre of 2 ½ million Jews in Europe, was correct. But, at this moment, December 8, 1942, he expressed that nothing could be done about this tragedy. The American Jewish leadership left the White House speechless; hardly anyone said a word. Adolf Held of the Jewish Labor Committee, one of the participants in this gathering, recorded these minutes of the meeting:

The meeting with the President was arranged for Tuesday, December 8, 1942, at 12 o'clock. We were originally notified that the President would give us 15 minutes, but the conference lasted 29 minutes....

When we were seated, the President opened the conversation by saying: "I am a sadist, a man of extreme sadistic tendencies. When I appointed Governor Lehman as head of the new Office of Relief and Rehabilitation, I had some very sadistic thoughts in my head. I know that Governor Lehman is a great administrator, and I wanted a great administrator for this post. I had another thought in my mind, however. I had hopes that, when God spares my life and the war is over, to be able to go to Germany, stand behind a curtain and have the sadistic satisfaction of seeing some 'Junkers' on their knees, asking Lehman for bread. And, by God, I'll urge him to give it to them"....

Rabbi Wise did not read the details of the Committee's statement but simply said: "Mr. President, we also beg to submit details and proofs of the horrible facts. We appeal to you, as head of our government, to do all in your power to bring this to the attention of the world and to do all in your power to make an effort to stop it."

The President replied: <u>"The government of the United States is very well acquainted with most of the facts you are now bringing to our attention. Unfortunately we have received confirmation from many sources. Representatives of the United States government in Switzerland and other neutral countries have given us proof that confirm the horrors discussed by you.</u> [Emphasis mine.] We cannot treat these matters in normal ways. We are dealing with an insane man – Hitler, and the group that surrounds him represent an example of a national psychotic case. We cannot act toward them by normal means. That is why the problem is very difficult. At the same time, it is not in the best interests of the Allied cause to make it appear that the entire German people are murderers or are in agreement with what Hitler is doing. <u>There must be in Germany elements, now thoroughly subdued, but who at the proper time will, I am sure, rise, and protest against the atrocities, against the whole</u>

Hitler system. *[Emphasis mine.]* *It is too early to make pronouncements such as President Wilson made, may they even be very useful. As to your proposal, I shall be glad to issue another statement, such as you request."*

The President turned toward the delegation for suggestions. All, except Rabbi Rosenberg, put in suggestions. Mine was about the possibility of getting some of the neutral representatives in Germany to intercede on behalf of the Jews. The President took notice of that but made no direct replies to the suggestions. The entire conversation on the part of the delegation lasted only a minute or two. As a matter of fact, of the 29 minutes spent with the President, he addressed the delegation for 23 minutes.

....We rose from our seats, and as we stood up, the President said: "Gentlemen, you can prepare the statement. I am sure that you will put the words into it that express my thoughts. I leave it entirely to you. You may quote from my statement to the Mass-Meeting in Madison Square Garden some months ago, but please quote it exactly. We shall do all in our power to be of service to your people in this tragic moment."

[Adolf Held, Memorandum: Report of the Visit to the President; File: Communication with the White House, Pt.3, Sec.1, #15, 1942; Jewish Labor Committee Archives.]

In the Fall of 1943, Hillel Kook decided that it was time to take strong measures to destroy that silence, which by the way he had been trying to do from early 1943. Moving from one event to another, just before the Jewish Day of Atonement on October 6, 1943, Hillel arranged and organized a march to Washington of approximately four-hundred Orthodox Jewish rabbis. The intention of the march was to alert the FDR Administration to the urgency of the Nazi exterminations, and to request that it take steps to help stop the massacre of European Jewry. Such an event, never before seen in Washington, was the brainchild of Hillel. Try to imagine convincing four-hundred Orthodox rabbis to march on Washington, on the eve of Yom Kippur no less – such an event had never been done before and has never been repeated since! The rabbis' goal of presenting a petition to Roosevelt to save European Jewry was not successful -- President Roosevelt simply slipped out of the White House in order not to meet with them.

It is important to present here the reaction of the American Zionist establishment to this event. The following piece is a translation from the Hebrew of an article in the magazine *Bitzaron* published in New York City at the end of 1943. The article was written as a response to the Orthodox rabbis' demonstration in Washington, D.C., which had been organized by Hillel Kook (in this article referred to as "a little child"), and is quoted here:

Our great Rabbis, the Titans, the "Rabbis of All the Diaspora, the Dwellers in this Sacred Community," their honored holinesses the Admors and the assorted saints and all the sacred vessels, the Cherethites and Pelethites and all their retinue, have suddenly abandoned their Rabbinical thrones; they girded their loins and curled their earlocks and trimmed their beards and went up to Washington, D.C. like a wall with their young and their old; and they filled the streets of Washington with the noise of their Psalms and prayers and shouting; and they prayed at the grave of Lincoln (May his merit protect us!) and walked upright in the crown, step by step, in the manner of Torah scholars. And all the people saw the thunder and lightning and their dignified faces and their kaftans, and the holy cloaks of the Great of Israel – and the people saw and they moved and stood afar, and shook their heads and envied the glory of Israel and its great majesty, for, thank God, they have greatness (rav). And not just one Rav, but several hundred Rabbonim, all heroes in the wars of Torah. Happy is the eye that has seen this! So they went, with a little child leading them [i.e., Peter H. Bergson], *until they reached the gate of the King and the Vice King. Once they had reached the King's Gate they felt at ease, for after all, they are like one of the family when it comes to the King's Gate (Shaar haMeleckh) and the Viceroy (Mishneh laMeleckh), the famous commentaries on Maimonides; the rest should be a small matter. But here their luck ran out; they found the gate of the King locked and shut before them, as if there is, God forbid, no honor for Torah, no honor for wisdom or age; even saying Psalms didn't help. The President sent his servant to tell them that "the man is not at home." Meaning what? That he has no need right now for responsa on the permitted and prohibited or on money matters; for these he certainly has other Poskim upon whom he relies in theory and in practice. And so they left in low spirits and went to the Viceroy, who is known as a man of faith and religion; the latter went out to them because of the honor of Torah, and shook his head and sighed because of the Exile of the Shechinah, and revealed to them a secret – that there is now a World War in progress and, God willing, after the war there will be peace in the world so that Judah will in any event be saved and Israel dwell securely.*

With this was ended the power of the Torah of the Rabbonim and they returned each one to his sackcloth and fasting and the four cubits of halakha and the <u>King's Gate</u> and <u>Viceroy</u> on Maimonides, over which they have more power than over the corresponding phenomena in Washington, D.C.

Well, after the President and anyone with any power to protest had been visited by any number of delegations and all types of *associations in the name of <u>all</u> Israel and <u>individual</u> Jews, and in the name of all disasters and all sorts of sects and parties, and after the representatives of the entire Jewish community went to see whomever there was to see in the name of all the American Jewry, the Rabbonim suddenly remembered that if they are here, everything is here, and if they aren't, then who is? They recalled that they are the genuine representatives of the Jewish people, and everything till now is simply non-existent. Oh how naïve are our knowledgeable and incisive Rabbonim! These "titans" did not sense or feel that behind them stand "pigmies" seekers of many accounts and that they used the Rabbis like toys. Some have an account to settle with the professional leadership which has kept them on the outside; some have arguments against the <u>Jewish organization</u> that did not invite them to the feast; and there are just plain publicity hunters, who like to fulfill "much confusion among them cast" and believe that loudness is good for the Jews, and that God is present in the noise; and, by the way, there is also the well-known phrase about "fasting, voice and money," for while this is going on one can also set up a plate and label it "Tzadaka of Tzeaka" ("The Shout of Charity"). And while these fellows are "busting their heads" – who will do the going? Where will they take the noisemakers, cymbals and horns? They* *saw the bargain and fell on it. We have, thank God, Rabbonim in the hundreds; they have the robes – let them be our captains. They have fur hats and silk kaftans and girdles and other priestly vestments upon which Washington's eye has never gazed. Psalms they know, thank God, by heart, traveling expenses can be taken care of – let's whistle for them to come, and they will be the delegated mouths of thy people Israel! And so, this calf emerged. The Rabbonim, may they live long, don't like to ask questions, after all, they are used to being asked questions. If you ask: did not Moses himself answer the Holy One, as it were: "If the children of Israel did not listen to me, how will Pharaoh listen to me, when I am uncircumcised of lips." Well, that's a verse in the Bible, and we all know that one does not decide halakha based on a Biblical verse.*

No doubt many of the Rabbonim expected the President to receive them as the legitimate leaders of the nation and when their voices would be heard in the White House the children of Israel will argue a "forterioro" and listen to their counsel and follow it, so that from this day on they would be representatives of the House of Israel in every place, and the Reform and semi-Reform "Rabbis" would no longer have access to the Senate and the White House. But many are the thoughts of the human heart and God did not think it best; their counsel was annulled and their plan went bad. The head of Aggudat Yisrael himself found the door shut before and all his pleas that "I am Solomon" didn't help; the guardians of the threshold did not permit him to enter. In short the Rav's, the titans and saints and all their retinue returned as low-spirited as they had come and all was as before. The so-called "Rabbis" will decide questions in the White House and the Rabbonim will decide questions in the slaughterhouse.

Our Rabbonim know the Talmud but one tractate they have forgotten or never learned: the tractate Dereckh Eretz (common courtesy). They did not know and didn't understand that Washington cannot be taken by storm. They should have known that there are specific keys to the White House, keys to the outside and the inside and the inner sanctum, and that those keys are in the hands of others. It's a rule: whoever has prepared on Friday will eat on Sabbath. They certainly know that when Zionism was in grave danger it was not they who asked mercy, that the evil decree be torn. It was a so-called "Rabbi" who always stands in the breach, in whose hands and in the hands of whose colleagues the keys to the kingdom's gate have been given. I ask about the Rabbonim, some of whom are, after all, clever in worldly matters too, and who know that there is an organization speaking in the name of all Jews (and some of them are members of it), that

> *this <u>organization</u> has already sent delegations to the rulers to speak in the name of the Jews – why did the Rabbonim suddenly gird their loins like warriors and set off to Washington? Was it not their intention to hint there, that the acts of the organization are null and void, that their representatives are not the genuine spokesmen of Israel but rather <u>we are</u>? However you look at it: if they regard themselves as knowledgeable in matters of the world and as leaders of the nation, how did they permit themselves to go after "blind goat" organizers to the President, without being certain beforehand that the President would receive them? Do they not feel the desecration of God's Name and the honor of the Torah? If the Rabbonim demand respect for Torah from the Jewish people, let them first be concerned for their own attitude, before they complain about that of the people.*
>
> *If the Torah Rabbis thought the streets of Washington would return them the power of Torah they had lost on the Jewish streets, this demonstration should prove to them their bitter mistake.*

I found an even more interesting, and to say the least ironic, response to the Rabbis' March on Washington in the archives of the World Jewish Congress. Nahum Goldmann, along with Rabbi Stephen Wise, met with Judge Samuel Rosenman, who was Roosevelt's speechwriter and one of his closest advisors and assistants. Rosenman also happened to be a prominent New York Jew. Dr. Goldmann wrote some notes about their conversation beginning with the following:

Judge Rosenman said he had seen the President that morning. The President was disturbed by the advertisement in the Washington Post this morning inserted by the Emergency Committee for the Rescue of European Jews. Judge Rosenman thought that these ads were doing a great deal of harm and the time had come for the responsible Jewish groups to come out with a statement, if necessary through an advertisement making it clear that they have no connection with the Jewish Army Committee group or its statements. Such a statement should be issued either on behalf of the Zionists or the American Jewish Conference and sent to Senators and Congressmen informing them that responsible Jewish groups are not behind the Army Committee or its statements.

Another compelling witness to White House events on October 6, 1943, was William D. Hassett. In his book *Off the Record with FDR, 1942-1945*, Hassett posts this entry from his diary:

October 6, Wednesday. *A full and varied day's program was behind the President when he left for Hyde Park tonight. A delegation of several hundred Jewish rabbis sought to present him a petition to deliver the Jews from persecution in Europe, and to open Palestine and all the United Nations to them. The President told us in his bedroom this morning he would not see their delegation; he told McIntyre to receive it. McIntyre* *said he would see four only – out of five hundred. Judge Rosenman, who with Pa Watson also was in the bedroom, said the group behind this petition not representative of the most thoughtful elements in Jewry. Judge Rosenman said he had tried -- admittedly without success -- to keep the horde from storming Washington. Said the leading Jews of his acquaintance opposed this march on the Capitol.*

By the end of 1943, another confrontation with Roosevelt was unfolding, but this time it took a different form and shape. Hillel had been in the United States for just over three years. He had accumulated defeats, but had also developed connections. Towards November 1943, he was beginning to move his compass-needle to the US Congress. The seeds of the plan that he had begun to formulate earlier that year at the Hotel Commodore were coming to fruition, as several Congressmen and Senators were prepared to propose a concurrent resolution before the Congress in order to put pressure on the President of the United States to take some action on behalf of European Jewry. Of course, this was a bold move on Hillel's part, but one must look at this action from the point of view of accumulated experiences, as well as of desperation. Something had to be done to focus on saving whatever was left of European Jewry! This story, which I will relate next, pivots on how to convince the President of the United States, in the middle of a World War, to take some action to save Jews. This is a very tragic story, a very tragic American story, and of course a very sad story about American

Jewish leadership -- a story, however, that must be told.

The concurrent resolution was presented in both Houses of Congress on November 9, 1943. Representatives Will Rogers, Jr., a Democrat from California, and Joseph C. Baldwin, a Republican from New York, presented it in the House of Representatives; Senator Guy Gillette, a Democrat from Iowa, Senator Elbert Thomas, a Democrat from Utah, Senator Edwin Johnson, a Democrat from Colorado, and several others of Kook's supporters presented it in the Senate. In the House of Representatives, the leading Congressman, the Chairman of the Foreign Relations Committee Sol Bloom, a New York Jew representing the Upper West Side of Manhattan, made utmost efforts to delay and kill the resolution. He called upon a variety of witnesses who basically said nothing to further the cause of rescue. In my view, Bloom represented the worst in Jewish hypocrisy and evil: a Congressman who tried to defend the State Department and its inactivity and obstructionism surrounding any attempts to save Jews. And of course, Bloom wanted the resolution to be dead. I think we need a crew of psychiatrists with many years of experience to figure out Representative Sol Bloom. It is difficult to comprehend why a Jewish Congressman from New York would stand to delay and destroy a resolution that might result in saving Jewish lives. After all, this resolution was no more than a recommendation for the President of the United States to act; instead, Bloom turned the hearing into a circus. Bloom invited Hillel Kook to be a witness when he was sitting as a spectator in the audience. He asked Hillel irrelevant questions, and tried to embarrass him by asking questions about his status in America. This hearing was obviously purposely conducted by Sol Bloom to obstruct the efforts to save European Jews. A good American playwright might find in this hearing boundless material for a great American play! A short quote from this hearing reveals something of the drama, as Mr. Bergson (Hillel Kook) responds to the question of a Congressman, in which he emphasizes the tragedy being suffered by European Jews:

Mr. Mundt. Do you mean that you intend to keep these people in camps?

Mr. Bergson. No; just a moment, please. Organize a reservation camp and make it known throughout Europe that every Jew who flees Europe, who flees death – because every Jew in Europe is facing death daily – and arriving at the border will be admitted into one these reservation camps. These camps combined could hold about 200,000 people. First of all, therefore, this camp could be instrumental in saving 200,000 people. Later we propose that this commission at this point – once the people are out, Mr. Chairman, they fall under the jurisdiction of the Intergovernmental Committee on Refugees – at this point I am in full agreement with the chairman that there is sufficient provision in the Intergovernmental Committee to act on this problem. Then those people are refugees. They are people who live in camps. It is very uncomfortable; it is crowded; they are not very productive; they have to *be put to work; they have to be taken somewhere; they are refugees. <u>Today the Jews are not!</u> [My emphasis.] Mr. Chairman, what they were called in London, namely, <u>potential refugees; they are potential corpses.</u> [My emphasis.]*

But let us return for a moment to explore a very important issue, namely, American Zionism. American Zionism was not acting normally during World War II, and I must again emphasize that its behavior was an echo of Palestinian Zionism. What did American Zionists do during the Holocaust? To better understand the problems American Jewry faced at the end of 1943, I am inserting here a Commentary written by Rabbi Dr. Isaac Lewin that might elucidate some of the tragic behavior demonstrated by the American Jewish leadership at this time. To quote in full:

"Indeed your blood, of your souls, I shall seek"

What is happening now in America with regard to saving Jews – goes beyond any measure and limit. It is a social scandal the likes of which have not been heard, one which will never be atoned for.

The blood of our miserable brethren in Europe has become like a ball used in a game by our so-called political leaders here. The blood of European Jewry is a "commodity" much sought after by the merchants. They want to hammer in the nails and build various palaces on the destruction of our people.

There was a united committee [the Joint Emergency Committee For European Jewish Affairs]. *To be sure, the actions of this committee were insufficient. At every meeting we called for greater acts. We aroused people, sometimes entreating, sometimes rebuking and shaming, to the point that this matter overrides all, that one should forget and neglect all questions and concern ourselves day and night with the saving of Jewry. If, to our sorrow, the United Committee* [mentioned above] *failed to do a third or a quarter of what it could have, it did, in any event, serve as a platform, where the representatives of the G-d-fearing Zionists, laborists and assimilationists could meet to seek counsel regarding the terrible destruction in Europe.*

This committee has been abrogated by the demand of the representatives of the Jewish Congress and the Zionist Federation. The reason was that the American Jewish Conference is supposed to deal with saving Jews. Representatives of Agudat Israel, Jewish Labor Committee, and American Jewish Committee strove mightily against this, but to no avail. Dr. Wise and his colleagues shut their ears to our arguments.

When I demanded at the Pittsburgh meeting [January 1943] *that the American Jewish Conference include the matter of saving European Jewry in their convention program – they refused. "The convention was called for a different purpose" –* declared the chairman Monsky [President of B'nai B'rith], *and declined even to pass my motion for a vote. Thus states the stenographic protocol of the Pittsburgh meeting. Now, with the convention behind us, and tremendous opposition aroused, their leaders have suddenly discovered that there is a topic in the world called "saving European Jewry." So they decided to "annex" this issue* [end of 1943]. *The name of the American Jewish Conference must be given to the work of saving the Jews – so they declared explicitly, and in order to reach this goal – the united committee must go out of existence.*

Several weeks have passed since the demise of the united committee. What has the American Jewish Conference done during this time to save our brethren in the bloody lands? We have heard nothing.

There was a discussion in the Foreign Relations Committee of the House of Representatives on the proposal of Reps. Rogers and Baldwin to create a special agency of the American government to deal with saving the Jews. This proposal was worked up by the Emergency Committee to Save the Jewish People of Europe [the Bergson Group], *and no doubt was a great achievement. However, Dr. Stephen Wise came before the committee and declared there was no substance to the proposal of Reps. Rogers and Baldwin since the important thing is to open the gates of Palestine. The "New York Times," the most influential paper in America, ran his statement the next day and from the press release it was obvious how Dr. Wise's words made a hard impression. And here one asks: If the gates to Palestine were open for all the Jews of the world – would Hitler refrain from killing the Jews? And if the American House of Representatives was aroused by non-Jewish members to deal with the question of Jewish survival – is it permissible for anyone to mix in with other questions, be they the most important? The members of the Foreign Relations Committee asked Dr. Wise serious questions about the Arabs, etc. and one can easily imagine how the issue of saving Jews was damaged by Dr. Wise's distracting them from it. G-d of Abraham, are his eyes blind to the fact that if there are, G-d forbid, no Jews in Europe, there will be nobody to go up to Palestine? Was he not concerned for the shame of displaying before the House of Representatives of the United States the fact that, even when it comes to saving the remnant, there is no unity in Israel, and what one builds the other dismantles, what one favors the other denies!*

More than this we learnt from the Revisionists [Lewin was mistaken here in referring to the Bergson Group as Revisionists] *at the press conference. They claim that two representatives of the American Jewish Conference had previously beseeched the proposing Congressmen and some Senators to desist from their motion and not speak with the "representatives of the Hebrew people"* [Bergson Group] *before they propose anew! Is this not a terrible shame and desecration?*

Indeed now we may understand the words of our Holy Torah in the section <u>Noah</u>: *"Indeed your blood, of your souls I shall seek; from every beast I shall seek and from man, from the hand of each man's brother, I shall seek the life of man" (Genesis 9:5). "From the hand of each man's brother" – this is what is happening now. G-d will seek the blood of our miserable brothers not only from the Nazi beast, from the hand of Hitler's murderers (may their name be erased!), but also from "each man's brother," from those who, instead of being brothers in calamity, are making politics out of the destruction of our people, from the hand of those who cause damage to the saving of Israel by introducing political matters into our struggle for survival!*

This is not the way.

[Reprint of a Commentary by Rabbi Dr. Isaac Lewin originally appearing in Hebrew in the magazine *HaPardes* 17:9 (December 1943), pp. 31-32.]

I met Rabbi Lewin in the mid-1970's, and he was still shaken up over what had happened during 1943 in America.

Hillel Kook, out of frustration with the approach taken by the American Jewish leadership, wrote a very important letter to Adolf Held, the president of the Jewish Labor Committee, reproduced here:

EMERGENCY COMMITTEE TO SAVE
THE JEWISH PEOPLE OF EUROPE
1 EAST 44TH STREET; NEW YORK 17,
N.Y.   MURRAY HILL 2-7237
31st of December 1943

Mr. Adolph Held
President, Jewish Labor Committee
175 East Broadway
New York City

Dear Mr. Held,

When the Senate Foreign Relations Committee unanimously adopted the resolution providing for the establishment of a specific commission to save the Jewish People of Europe – a favorable situation at last was created which promises to lead to large-sale government measures to save these otherwise doomed people.

But in this favorable hour, a paradoxical situation is still permitted to continue which confuses and therefore weakens the efforts of all who should unite their strength in the interest of the helpless.

While prominent American figures, and leading American newspapers of all shades of political opinion, have urged the immediate passage of the Congressional resolution, and while every independent Jewish-American newspaper and magazine in the country has enthusiastically heralded the demands for this resolution, some Jewish organizations have remained strangely non-committal, silent or actually obstructive. Worse than that: the leaders of some influential American-Jewish organizations have found it opportune, in this moment of greatest emergency and catastrophe for the Jewish people abroad, to start a fight amongst themselves – even to the extent of attacking the initiators of this non-sectarian and non-partisan movement.

The situation is not only strange and paradoxical, it is tragic. This letter is written not to criticize or blame; it is written with the fervent hope that even at this late hour, all of the resources and energies of the leading

Jewish organizations in this country will strive to mobilize for one concerted effort to secure action by the United States and the United Nations. For only through such action can we hope to save countless people from certain death.

We must keep before us just one grim fact – we must rescue Jews who are about to die. If they are allowed to die, their blood will be on our hands, for there can be no greater sin against God or man than to permit divergence of opinion on internal political questions among Jewish-American groups to affect the rescue of millions of Jews in Europe.

The Palestinian Delegation associated with this committee has always most carefully and studiously avoided all problems dealing with communal or organizational life of Jews in this country. In the opinion of this Delegation, the problem of saving the Jews of Europe and the general or internal problems of the Jews in this country must be kept distinctly apart.

We have aimed to organize a movement, on a strictly non-partisan and non-sectarian basis, for the sole purpose of saving those who need and expect our help. We appeal for understanding and for help to the American people -- 135,00,000 strong. However, we recognize that the help of the Jewish organizations is of utmost importance. Such help and cooperation need not in the least affect the regular activities of Jewish organizations. It is difficult to conceive of a situation in which two Jewish-American organizations cannot agree to discuss plans for the salvation of the Jews of Europe -- merely because they do not agree on the structure of the Jewish community in this country, or the future of Palestine. That is why we consider the dissolution of the Joint Emergency Committee on European-Jewish Affairs, because of internal organizational divergences among Jewish-Americans, a tragic misconception of the catastrophic situation of European Jewry.

History will judge guilty all who refuse to put aside their political prejudices, to the neglect of a most urgent and most sacred task -- the rescue of the remaining Jews of Europe. From the ghastly regions of torture and slaughter in Eastern Europe have come messages which boil down to a horrifying curse on the heads of American Jewry -- "We hate you!" We cannot, we must not permit this tragic situation to continue.

We, therefore, most earnestly appeal to you to participate in a meeting next Thursday, 8:30 P.M., January 6th at the Lotus Club, 110 West 57th Street, which we have taken the initiative of calling in order to present to you a plan of rescue and an outline of the way in which all Jewish-American organizations can unite behind it. We are not attempting to create "unity" between Jewish organizations: the internal political arguments and fights will most probably continue as before, but they will be separate for once and for all from the campaign to save the Jews of Europe, and thus they will not be carried out at the expense of other Jewish lives.

Surely no possible harm can come from such a meeting; perhaps some good. We shall, therefore, be looking forward to meeting with you at this conference devoted to considering just one great problem – rescue.

Very truly yours,
Mr. Peter H. Bergson
    Dr. Maurice William
Co-Chairman
    Chairman, Executive Board

EMERGENCY COMMITTEE TO SAVE THE JEWISH PEOPLE OF EUROPE

From 1943 until the end of the War, the American Zionists wasted time. The American Zionist leadership tried to unify American Jewry behind their Zionist banner so that after the War they would be able to act as a large political body to convince whomever would be President of the US to establish a political entity in Palestine. What kind of a political entity they would call for is not clear. And now in the Congress, in the midst of an attempt to pass a resolution to save the remnant of European Jewry, Representative Sol Bloom, who called himself a "Zionist" whenever it was convenient for him to do so, asked Rabbi Stephen Wise to appear as a witness. When Hillel worked to convince Congressmen and Senators to pursue the resolution to save the remnant of European Jewry, he made a deliberate decision not to mention Palestine in the resolution. He did so purposely: it was not that Palestine did not play a very important role in his political life, or that he suddenly abandoned Zionism. He made this decision because any time the word "Palestine" was mentioned in any proposal to save Jews, the proposal was doomed to fail. Then, this elderly Reform rabbi, Stephen Wise, in a not-so-wise moment, appeared at the hearing to express his unwillingness to support the rescue resolution because it did not mention Palestine. I do not want to analyze the Zionists' approach. However, despite the public statements of Zionist officials, Hillel's friends and supporters especially in the Senate, specifically Senator Elbert Thomas from Utah, managed to pass a resolution in the Senate Foreign Relations Committee which they readied to present before the entire Senate.

Many historians have dealt with this period of time, including with what came about after the arguments on Capitol Hill at the end of 1943, and eventually with the creation of the War Refugee Board in early 1944. It is worthwhile mentioning that before and during the hearing, Hillel developed a very close relationship with one of the lawyers who worked in the office of the Secretary of the Treasury. His name was Josiah DuBois, Jr. Dubois was very involved in persuading Treasury Secretary Henry Morgenthau, Jr., to approach Roosevelt and demand that he act to save Jews. Here we have another development that is rather significant: Treasury Secretary Morgenthau, who was a personal friend of Roosevelt, received a document in his office that revealed the efforts and obstacles concocted by the State Department in order to disrupt and prevent action for the rescue of European Jews by the United States Government. Finally, as a result of the pressure that was building up in different places -- including the Congress, the Treasury and public opinion -- President Roosevelt announced the creation of the War Refugee Board on January 22, 1944.

Here I would like to bring in a few short notes on some other aspects of Hillel Kook's work in the year 1943. While focusing on the effort to convince the US Government to confront the ongoing massacre of European Jewry, he also undertook a few other things. The first among these was to send Ariyeh Ben Eliezer to Palestine in an attempt to revive and restructure the Irgun. This restructuring would contribute in part to the revolt against British policies during WWII. This restructuring also resulted in the installation of Menachem Begin as the new leader of the Irgun. I am not going to enter here into details of this story; there is plenty of literature available on it. Hillel, in thinking back about sending Ben Eliezer to Palestine to revive the Irgun, summed up his own action many years later as one of the most disastrous in his life. As it subsequently turned out, Begin had no clue or understanding or respect for the political work done by Hillel in the United States during this critical period. Next, another issue Hillel dealt with in 1943 was how to rid himself of the pressure placed upon him by the Zionists and other Jewish organizations, who criticized the Bergson Group over why they were not actively engaged in joining the war defense effort. For this reason he sent Ben Ami and Hadani to join the US Army. Later on, when they both returned from the War, they helped to carry out missions to Palestine and other places, which they were able to do because they had acquired US citizenship in the process. And to conclude, this basically sums up some of Hillel's side activities in 1943.

However, I must continue by including four additional critical aspects of this story. One was definitely thought about at the end of 1943, and a second was what happened at the end of 1943 and early 1944. Also, another event happened on Broadway in New York in 1946, plus another one in 1948.

While dealing with a variety of issues concerning European Jews, some of Hillel's thoughts centered around the future of the political status of Jews. It was clear to him from the beginning of the War that the Jews who had been caught up in the claws of the Nazis had lost their political status as citizens, and thus became the victims of a regime that wanted them to be dead. So the political status of these Jews both during the War and afterwards bothered Hillel. His conclusion that he must act on behalf of the *political* status of European Jews crystalized after the announcement of the establishment of the War Refugee Board in January 1944. While the creation of the War Refugee Board was largely secured by Hillel's work in Washington in 1943, the result of this Board was in fact a disaster. For the issue was not Refugees! Jewish people were being exterminated! The US Government needed to make a clear statement that it wanted to save Jews, but that did not happen. The Government's choice of the term "Refugee" Board avoided stating that this was an agency established to save Jews, even though this was its real mission. This ambiguity caused Hillel huge frustration, and this frustration, along with other factors connected to his activities that came into play, led Hillel to another strategic conclusion. His line of thinking was apparently as follows: since the goal of the Irgun was to be a National Liberation movement, and that is what it was in reality, if a nation was to be created after the War, that nation would have to have a name, a name that would define its nationality. This concept of defining the new nation by its nationality likely came to mind to Hillel from a book written by Jabotinsky that appeared in Palestine in 1937. The book, titled *A Hebrew Nation: The Solution to the Question of the Jews*, was a short book, confusing to many, but in my view it should be seen as the guideline to what Hillel decided to do in Washington from early 1944 until 1948. For as money was collected as a result of the campaign to save European Jews, especially from the middle of 1943, Hillel decided by the end of 1943 on a bold step: he purchased a building in Washington, DC, the purpose of which would be to serve as a Hebrew Embassy for the people of the Hebrew Nation! In May, 1944, the Hebrew Embassy officially opened and flew the flag of the Hebrew Nation -- the same flag that the Israelis adopted in 1948.

The American Zionist Movement went ballistic over the opening of the Embassy. The following letter written by Arthur Lourie, Secretary of the American Zionist Emergency Council, to the United States Department of State, circa the end of 1944, explains the Zionists' frustration over this bold move of Hillel's in establishing the Hebrew Embassy:

<u>Memorandum on the Hebrew Committee of National Liberation:</u>

[This document was given to me in 1979 by Yitshaq Ben-Ami, who received it from the US State Department under the Freedom of Information Act.

The essence of Lourie's letter is to condemn and ridicule the Hebrew Committee of National Liberation as an unworthy representative of Jews. Following are annotated excerpts of this letter.]

****

...4. It is in these circumstances that a body styling itself the "Free Palestine Committee," a name later changed to "The Hebrew Committee of National Liberation," has of very recent months come forward in this country and claims recognition on behalf

of the "Hebrew people of Europe and Palestine."

Who are the members of this committee? They are the same "handful" (to use their own term) of Palestinians, under the leadership of Mr. Peter Bergson, who have been responsible for a series of paper organizations in the past few years, including the "American Friends of a Jewish Palestine," the "Committee for a Jewish Army of Stateless and Palestinian Jews," the "Emergency Conference," and the "Emergency Committee to Save the Jewish People of Europe," and the "American League for a Free Palestine." Not merely is this group without any democratic basis of election in this country, but it is utterly unrepresentative of the Jews of Palestine, where they amount so far as public life is concerned, to the fragment of a fragment. They are associated with a small terrorist group called the "Irgun Zvai Leumi," whose activities have been condemned and repudiated not only by the National Council of the Jews of Palestine and by the Jewish Agency, but by the entire Jewish press in Palestine as well as by the Jewish press in this country from the extreme right to the extreme left. Their object has been, and remains, to destroy the existing Zionist leadership by any and every means and to place themselves in control of Zionist affairs.

5. The "Hebrew Committee of National Liberation" and its supporting body "The American League for a Free Palestine," has developed an ideology premised upon an alleged distinction between American Jews and all other Jews. American Jews are merely "Americans of Hebrew descent" other Jews are the "Hebrew people of Europe and Palestine." Apart from the patent nonsense of this distinction, it also has grave implications; for the inference is that while there is no distinction between Jews and non-Jews so far as American citizenship is concerned, the Jews of Europe, as members of a separate "Hebrew Nation," have no claim to citizenship in the countries where they live. The Zionist movement believes in and fights for the right of such Jews as wish to go to Palestine to go there, but it also believes in and will fight for the right of <u>full</u> <u>and</u> <u>equal</u> <u>citizenship</u> for Jews in <u>any</u> country where they may live. In denying this right to the Jews of Europe, Mr. Bergson and his associates do harm not merely to European Jewry, but also ultimately and inevitably to Jews everywhere, including the Jews of America. Justice to the Jewish people demands the establishment of a Jewish homeland, and in order that that homeland may not become another temporary center for refugees, our goal must be the establishment of a democratic Jewish

Commonwealth in Palestine. But this no more affects the whole-hearted political allegiance of American Jews to America than of Jews elsewhere to the countries where they live. To suggest otherwise is as irresponsible as it is dangerous, and for Mr. Bergson and his associates to pretend that they speak on behalf of the "Hebrew" people of Europe is nothing but political charlatanism. There are many representatives of European Jewry in this country, some of them organized in the World Jewish Congress, who are in a position, if anyone is in a position, to voice the sentiments of the silenced Jewry of Europe; we have still to hear that they have given their allegiance to or recognized Mr. Bergson as their spokesman.

...To sum up, the Hebrew Committee of National Liberation stands for ideas, which, insofar as they are new are dangerous; and insofar as they are not new are being effectively pursued by other well-established and well-recognized bodies. The Committee consists of a small, self-constituted group, altogether without any popular democratic base and responsible to no one; it is linked with elements condemned by every section of Jewish life, and its efforts to achieve recognition as the spokesman of the Jews of Palestine and Europe can only lead to confusion and damage so far as the cause of a Jewish Palestine is concerned....

The Hebrew Embassy story is a bit complex, and I would like to elucidate here some surrounding issues of that bold attempt by Hillel in 1944. The year 1943 was over, and of course, like anything in the universe, it comprised a continuous stretch of events to the year 1944. But I want to concentrate here on the activities of Hillel Kook at the end of 1943. After a tumultuous year of trying desperately to save Jews, the old ideas embedded in him since his arrival in the US from Palestine in 1940 started kicking in again. For a variety of reasons, he started to review and take stock of the events of 1943, with the realization of defeat. Even amidst all his determination to respond quickly to the terrible situation in Europe, it became clear that any of his efforts to save European Jewry were almost futile. But because he had been able to move public opinion, and thus his organization had been able to collect money that was donated by the public, he started thinking about how best to invest that money for the future of European and Palestinian Jewry. With the help of his friends, Hillel purchased the house in Washington in early 1944 which he declared to be a "Hebrew Embassy." In May 1944, he raised the Hebrew National flag that had been born and designed in Palestine in the town of Rishon Lezion. The symbolism of such an act is not difficult to figure out: every nation has a flag. It is true that in the past 2000 years, Jews were not exactly a nation, but now in Washington in May, 1944, that status was to change with the presence of a Hebrew Embassy. Thus it is simultaneously true that in the past 2000 years Jews did not exist as a political entity, but now they had a Hebrew Committee of National Liberation. As a National Liberation movement, they had the right to claim representation as a nation under assault by two governments: the German and the British. This idea of national liberation is not completely unknown among modern nations, but when it came to Jews who did not have any nation for at least 2000 years, there was a problem, i.e., how to explain and justify that bold move by Hillel.

When I spent some time at the end of the 1970's discussing the Hebrew Nation concept with him, Hillel explained to me the reasons he thought it had been necessary for him to take the action he did in 1944. First, he said, was to give hope to Jews, especially in Europe, who could come to see that they finally had some political recognition, and that this political entity, the Hebrew Nation, was legitimized with its Embassy in Washington. Besides that element of hope, Hillel thought that he was spreading the idea of the Hebrew Embassy and Nation as a modern political tool that looked to him completely rational and appropriate in the modern age. In his desire to act responsibly, when the future goal was an independent Palestine, he unfortunately completely miscalculated the impact of his actions, because the American Jewish leadership, and especially the American Zionist leadership, were not ready for such a bold move.

I would like to introduce two explanations, written in those days by two writers who were associated with the Hebrew Committee of National Liberation, in order for the reader to grasp the gist of the issue. Both documents were published in 1945 by the American League for a Free Palestine, which was a public American support group formed by Hillel to enhance the idea of a Hebrew Nation:

Every struggle for national liberation, beginning with the revolt of the American Colonies, has seen the emergence of a group of patriots, who arbitrarily assumed authority and were eventually recognized as the spokesmen of their people....

One other point needs to be stressed. The members of the Hebrew Committee of National Liberation took the initiative in establishing a provisional national authority because they recognized that the existence of such a body spelled the difference between survival and extermination of the Hebrew People.

[Johan J. Smertenko, *Struggle for Life and Freedom: Background, Program and Activities of the Hebrew Committee of National Liberation*; Sponsored by the American League for a Free Palestine, 1945; pp.7 &11.]

The concept of a Hebrew nation makes clear and definite the relation between Palestine and the diaspora. It means an independent state but it likewise means complete social emancipation of the Jew as a citizen wherever he might be. The Hebrew state is to be the haven of safety and security for every Jew unable or unwilling to remain in diaspora.

[Isaac Zaar, *Hebrew Independence: The Contribution of the Hebrew Committee of National Liberation*; Published by the American League for a Free Palestine, 1945; p.41.]

Of course, the Israeli Nation that was born in 1948 had to deal exactly with the same issues that Hillel foresaw in 1944, ahead of Ben Gurion and his leadership in Palestine four years later. In 1948, when the opportunity arose to create a new nation, something funny happened: Ben Gurion, a long-time Socialist, suddenly did two things that reflect what Hillel already spoke about in 1944. Hillel had emphasized that when this new nation, which in his mind should be called a Hebrew Nation, would appear on the political scene, it would have to represent the people who declared and lived *within its sovereignty*, and not the entire body of Jews worldwide. Ben Gurion, influenced by ideas set forth by Hillel's Committee for National Liberation, set out to write a Declaration of Israeli Independence modeled after an American Jeffersonian concept as presented in the American Declaration of Independence. But probably due to his misunderstanding of what that Declaration meant, Ben Gurion's Declaration of Israeli Independence is one of the most absurd documents written. For in his Declaration, adopted by the new Nation, he apparently confused 2000 years of Jewish existence with a modern statement of a new Israeli Nation, confusing what was to be a political entity born in 1948 ostensibly to accommodate Israeli independence, to instead in essence declare the independence of worldwide Jewry.

The second more tragic issue was the fact that, despite Hillel's emphasis on the birth of a new *sovereign* nation, and it does not matter if it is named the Hebrew Nation or the Israeli Nation, Ben Gurion, not understanding the meaning of a modern Israeli nation as a sovereign nation, made sure that Israel wrote no constitution, contrary to what Hillel had strongly advocated as a way to define a modern nation. In his book *The Struggle for Statehood*, published in Hebrew in 1979, Eliyhu Eilat encapsulated the Bergson Group's philosophy of statehood by citing a conversation between David Stern, the owner of the *Philadelphia Record*, and President Harry S. Truman. In this conversation, the President had expressed his view that he was against the concept of a Jewish State in Palestine, the same way that he was against a Muslim state or a state of the Baptists. He went on to declare that the President supported opening the Gates of Palestine for Jews, Muslims and Christians, so that they could all live in a democratic state. Another interesting comment came from the Soviets in 1947 and can be found in Judd L. Teller's book, *Strangers and Natives*:

On October 13, 1947, announcing Moscow's reversal of previous policy and her readiness to support a Jewish state in a part of Palestine, Andrei Gromyko offered a rationale which corresponded to the definition which Bergson gave in 1944. The Jews outside Palestine have only a religion in common, the Palestinian Jews have all the characteristics of nationhood -- a common territory, a common language, a common economy. [p.205]

The fact that today Israel is trying officially to declare itself a Jewish State simply means that, after sixty-nine years, still nobody seems to understand what a modern Israeli nation means! This insistence on calling itself a Jewish Nation is the antithesis of the Jeffersonian Declaration of Independence, which Hillel tried, futilely, to bring to the modern nation. The United States of America is not called the United States of Christian America, and since the Israelis are not exactly sure who they are or what they stand for, they confuse themselves by calling themselves a Jewish Nation. This emphasis on preserving the term Jewish Nation is, I believe, the greatest obstacle for Israeli's survival.

When in 1944 Hillel created the Hebrew Committee of National Liberation, the entire Zionist organization attacked him, opening up a very complex issue going back 2000 years: Who has the right to speak on behalf of Jews? This is an issue that cannot be resolved in this essay. To wrap up this issue of the political identity of Jews, I would like to explore, though not in depth, two additional events that Hillel was involved in. But before that I must explain something: I think it would be responsible to say that Hillel's mind was evolving ever since his arrival as a child in Palestine. His growing up in Jerusalem, his association with the Irgun, his mission to Europe and his work in America indicate purpose and dedication on behalf of Jews. Keeping those experiences in mind, along with the urgent desire to create a Hebrew Republic, led him to do two things. One of them was to bring about a Broadway production, which was based on a play written by Ben Hecht. The play was called, "A Flag is Born." It is a story of survivors of the Holocaust with the scenes set in a graveyard in Europe, where a sort of resurrection comes about with a young survivor who decides to go to Palestine to fight for the new Hebrew Nation. The role of the young survivor was played by a young Marlon Brando, which was phenomenal in itself. Beyond that, it was Hillel, probably, who inserted into Hecht's play some lines that evoked American Jewish life in the Holocaust years. Hillel's assessment and response to what American Jews did during WWII were reflected in the play by the young Brando, who deeply moved the audiences. Here is what Marlon Brando said on stage in words written by Ben Hecht inspired by Hillel's thoughts:

Where were you -- Jews? Where were you when the killing was going on? When the six million were being burned and buried alive in the lime pits, where were you? Where was your voice crying out against the slaughter? We didn't hear any voice. There was no voice. You Jews of America! You Jews of England! Strong Jews, rich Jews, high-up Jews; Jews of power and genius! Where was your cry of rage that could have filled the world and stopped the fires? Nowhere! Because you were ashamed to cry out as Jews. You would rather let us die than speak out as Jews! A curse on your silence! That frightened silence of Jews that made the Germans laugh as they slaughtered. You with your Jewish hearts hidden in your American boots! You -- with your Jewish hearts hidden behind English accents -- you let the six million die -- rather than make the faux-pas of seeming a Jew. We heard -- your silence -- in the gas chambers. And now, now you speak a little. Your hearts squeak -- and you have a dollar for the Jews of Europe. Thank you. Thank you!

There was a compelling letter written by a Zionist supporter to one of the Zionist leaders in Philadelphia which I would like to quote here, as it rather exemplifies the tragic status of the Zionists in America during WWII:

February 6, 1947
Michael N. Egnal, Esq.
115 South Broad Street
Philadelphia, Pa.

Dear Mr. Egnal:
In reply to your letter of February 3rd, calling my attention to the Zionist Organization Celebration with dinner at the Bellevue-Stratford on March 12th, where you mention my annual contribution of $100.00, I wish to inform you that this particular contribution of $100.00 of mine will be given elsewhere this year.

While attending the Zionist meeting at the Benjamin Franklin hotel on January 27th, at least a dozen people approached me and pleaded not to attend the Play "A Flag is Born". I attended the play on Tuesday night and to my chagrin actual pickets were around the theatre with the following placards "Do not attend this play" -- "Watch your pockets" -- "Do not contribute as the money is being wasted".

Dear Mr. Egnal, is the Zionist Organization above criticism in reference to monies collected and spent? I have benefited more spiritually by this play than all the Zionist meetings I ever attended. It is a shame that a great number of timid souls heeded your idle gossip and innuendoes and stayed away from this masterful play, thus depriving Jewish leaders and artists of a well deserved income. You favored the sale of Palestinian securities and called a special meeting to that effect. This play portrays vividly the life and death and spirit of the present Jewish existence. There is no better piece of propaganda than this play. Do you realize that many non-Jewish people attended this play also? What an impression on them to witness the disgraceful display of disunion among Jews!!

I can hardly express myself adequately the bad taste and disgust I felt that night, and still do, of this nasty affair perpetrated in the name of the Zionist Organization of America.

In conclusion, I know you as an intelligent and arduous Zionist will realize the harm it has done to the organization both locally and nationally -- I am sure you are aware of the publicity in the New York papers.

Very truly yours,

Bernard L. Kahn M.D.

Another matter, again within the realm of Hillel's general understanding and philosophy of what should be done with the Hebrew Nation, by now the Israeli Nation, is the story of the tragic events surrounding the ship *Altalena*. The story of the ship is well known to many: it was an Irgun-sponsored ship, full of people and ammunition that arrived in Israel in June 1948, immediately following independence and with the full knowledge of the new Israeli government. Due to total confusion, or as I would like to say total misunderstanding, perhaps due to the belief that Hillel was on board, which he was not, the ship was bombed by the new Israeli Army as it stood close to the Tel Aviv beach. The entire episode is a sad story for which Hillel paid a heavy price. The Israeli Government authorities detained him on the beach north of Tel Aviv and were ready to kill him. To me there is no doubt that this murky event was the brainchild of Ben Gurion, who ordered the ship to be bombed, an act that appears to have been in retribution for Hillel's activities in the United States during WWII, which basically resulted in the ridiculing and undermining of the entire apparatus of the clueless Zionist Movement. So Hillel Kook, who fought to save European Jewry, when he finally arrived in Israel, ended up in an Israeli jail. Of course, that is not the end of his life story.

Following is a letter Hillel sent out from jail to his Israeli lawyer Max Seligman to explain the circumstances surrounding his arrest:

July 11, 1948

Mr. Max Seligman
Advocate
Tel Aviv

My dear Seligman,

I shall be grateful to you if you will convey to the public some facts connected with the moral aspect of my detention, not to speak of the alleged legality of my detention, if the British Emergency Regulations can be considered legal at all, and as far as it is possible to call the fabrication of "charges" and "suspicions" law and justice.

A Mr. Shiller, an American journalist, was brought before me, not at my request, and I readily agreed to speak to him and make a statement. I gave him a copy of a letter which I had written to Mr. Heftman and most of which was published in the newspaper "Haboker." The statement I made was on the basis of that letter. I hereby declare that at least 80% of what he later printed was written afterwards and was composed mainly of innovations and interpretations without any connection with what I had said. I would like particularly to deny the statement made in my name that I allegedly demanded the resignation of Menachem Begin. It is absurdity not worthy of being discussed.

I should like to emphasize that, several hours after the visit of Mr. Shiller, I was transferred from the good surroundings I had in the Kibbutz, to a prison where I was confined to a cell under conditions which the English prepared for Arab criminals. I requested that a journalist be brought to me. I even agreed to the same Mr. Shiller being brought in order that he should see the new conditions which are most severe and the aim of which is revenge and not detention.

The only charge which has so far been brought against me was that of being "suspected of intention to leave the country." Today there was read to me an order of detention issued against me under the Emergency Regulations of the British occupation. There are no words to express the feelings of ridicule and contempt which I have for those people who have desecrated the memory of our sacred dead. Not only the scores who were hanged and who fell during the British occupation, but also the thousands, including the soldiers of the Defense Army, who fell in the present war which is being conducted by the British and with their arms, money and officers.

And there is a further request which I have to make. Please address the friends of our people in America, friends without whose public and financial support we would have no existence in this country. Ask them to save our people from the fate of tyranny, concentration camps and other fascist attributes which now threaten our country.

Above all, I ask them to stop these crimes, these dastardly deeds of madness in war-time when we need to concentrate all the powers of our people for the defense of the country in order to save it from the military and political destruction which Bevin's men are preparing for us.

As regards the charges set out in the affidavit made by the Head of the Defense Army, I have to declare that his statements are untrue. I was not in Kfar Vitkin during the disturbances there. I left Kfar Vitkin on Monday, June 21st, in the afternoon, and I was already under arrest at 7:00. The disturbances commenced later. I also declare that I had no function in Kfar Vitkin, and I was there only as a visitor.

As regards my past, the Chief of Staff was entirely correct. I was arrested for that and it is for that that I am now detained. During my ten years of activity abroad for the country and its liberation, the English constantly tried to have me arrested and now the Chief of Staff has arrested me according to British desire and in accordance with

British-made laws. I was only arrested in revenge for my activities as a Member of the Hebrew Committee for National Liberation, for the freeing of Palestine, which was not in line with the will of the men of the Jewish Agency. But in my opinion, the use of arms of the Defense Army of Israel for revenge of this kind is an abuse of the oath which these soldiers have taken to be faithful to the people and country because it is for these that they swore and not for the men of the Agency.

(Signed) HILLEL KOOK

(Peter H. Bergson)

After a short while, Hillel was released from prison. He then joined the Herut Party, which was led by Menachem Begin, and he became a member of the first Israeli Knesset. During his time in the Knesset, Hillel tried his best to introduce and to argue for the central political American idea of a constitution for the new Israeli Nation. Ben Gurion opposed this idea, and Begin did not care much for it. In the end, Hillel left Israel in the early 1950's and returned to America, where he resided for the next twenty years before returning to Israel, where he lived out the remainder of his life.

Israel has all but forgotten Hillel Kook, and so has America. This short book is my attempt to revive some interest in the man, his activities, and his vision, for a future understanding of what happened in the Holocaust, and in its aftermath.

***

For many years while working in Manhattan, I was employed at a stationery store. The owner, who had a good sense of humor as well as an excellent business sense, would always look at the incoming customers and do a quick analytical review. Then he would subtly call out a code word to all his workers so that they would understand how to behave with this customer and how to serve him or her. For example, if the owner assessed the individual to be a criminal of some sort, he would call out "File Folder." This meant that the NY Police Department likely had a file on him. Hillel Kook's "file folder" at the FBI was as long as Broadway! In fact, it was not only the FBI that kept files on him, but other government agencies did the same. The voices of informants are very strong in these files, and most of these people worked for Jewish organizations. The reason for their informing against him was fundamentally their attempt to get rid of Kook, meaning that they wanted to ensure that the American investigating authorities would call for his deportation. But America is bigger than that. The connections that Hillel Kook developed with Congressmen, Senators and many other prominent Americans kept him in America, despite all the actions of the informants.

Why was Kook so despised and reviled by so many Jewish organizations? Hillel Kook, during his first eight years in the US, from 1940-1948, did what no other Jew did during WWII. He rigorously challenged the authorities of the United States and demanded, without fear, that the US Government take action to save European Jewry. He also called for an independent Hebrew Republic in Palestine. It should be obvious to historians and lay people alike that the United States of America was the only hope Jews had in WWII. American Jewish leaders from the far ideological left to the far ideological right were not exactly sure about how to deal with that conundrum; or, how to challenge the "common-sense" idea, or that there was a need to challenge the "common-sense" idea that nothing could be done unless "we win the War." Hillel Kook challenged the standard ideological Zionist thinking of creating a "Jewish" State. He maintained Judaism is not a Nationality; Judaism is a Religion. If modernity taught Hillel anything, it was that in order to become a modern nation, Israeli Jews would have to figure out another way of identifying themselves, so that they might survive in the future. Sadly, his idea of a Hebrew Republic with a written constitution never came to be.

Kook's work in America between 1940 and 1948, without a doubt paved the way for President Truman to recognize the Israeli Nation in 1948. Only a genius like Kook could come up with a slogan every American could understand and support: "It's 1776 in Palestine!" You Americans got rid of the British in 1776, and we are now beginning that same path in 1944 -- thus he opened the Hebrew Embassy in Washington.

So far, the study covered in this work in reality focuses on the year 1943, one of the most terrible years for European Jewry.

<u>Hillel, as I declared before, was, and forever will remain, I believe the most important Jewish figure in the past 2000 years</u> – it is very simple to figure this out.

The atrocity of the Holocaust was such as to demand leadership that would challenge authority and insist upon action. No other Jewish person stepped up and persevered to take on this urgent challenge. Of course, it is an "embarrassment" today to mention Kook's name. American Jews and their historians simply do not know how to write or speak about him. Israelis do not know much about him. Meanwhile, Israelis are moving from an "Israeli" nation of modern times to an increasingly parochial "Jewish" state. I wish someone could explain how Religion has suddenly become a Nationality.

I wrote this document primarily to raise public interest in a man, an individual, whom I met many years ago while doing research on American attitudes and actions during WWII vis-à-vis European Jews. I hope my work makes sense, or, if it does not make sense, that it will at least convince some people to reexamine their notions about the past and future of Jews. The survival of Israel and the Israelis depends on *Am Lo Levadad Ishkon*, meaning "a nation does not stand by itself." I understand that this concept is in contradiction to 2000 years of the history of the Jews. Unfortunately, sometimes the thinking has to change in order to move forward.

CHAPTER TWO

MODERN ISRAEL: ISRAEL AS A PHILOSOPHICAL PROBLEM, OR JUST A PUZZLE? AN INTERVIEW WITH HILLEL KOOK, A.K.A. PETER BERGSON

A cat has a thousand dreams, all about mice.
--An Arab Proverb

The following conversation between Hillel Kook, a.k.a. Peter Bergson, and myself took place in June, 1981. The location was a building on Madison Avenue in New York City near 76th Street on the fifth floor, where his office was located in those years. I worked for a short time in this office when I was finishing up my MA degree and beginning my efforts to write a doctoral dissertation. The majority of my research was focused on an historical analysis of the response of the American Jewish leadership to the Holocaust. I was working in conjunction with my former professor, David S. Wyman. This research was a continuation of the work being done by

Wyman that he had been engaged in for over twelve years and was in preparation for his upcoming book on the United States Government and the Holocaust. Dr. Wyman introduced me to Peter Bergson and encouraged me to speak with him.

I had first met Peter Bergson a few years prior to this recorded interview/conversation. As a result of previous meetings with him, I started getting interested in the connection between the Holocaust and the creation of the Israeli Nation. With Bergson's permission, I recorded this conversation, as well as many others. So while this conversation was not the only one I recorded, this particular conversation was extremely important because it gave me an opportunity to understand, more or less, his world vision. His psychological and spiritual condition was troubled; he was extremely depressed, and the conversation reflects that. At that time, I was not well aware of the extent of the severity of the problems that Bergson was talking about, or their implications. In 1982 I began writing a series of articles which, about thirty years later, I compiled into a short book titled "Who is an Israeli?" I dedicated the book to Hillel Kook, as well as to our son Michael for whom Hillel was his godfather. The material in this document that follows does not include the entire conversation we had at the time, but rather includes those parts of the conversation in which Hillel tried to clarify the issues surrounding the emergence of the Israeli Nation. The text is written as best I could record and transcribe his words.

HILLEL KOOK: The issue is, the problem is, that you need to separate Religion from Politics. This Israeli religious officer in the Army was speaking about religion in the Israeli army and the fact that he is religious. Then the father of this secular Israeli soldier responded. In my opinion, the secular father has no right to attack the opinions of the religious officer -- it is the right of an Orthodox person to believe that G-d promised him this land -- but let him talk about it as a religious issue, not as an issue that is connected to the military he serves in. It is not a legitimate argument in this context. I defend the right of the military officer, this religious person, but not in the framework of the military, only in the framework of a religious argument. What is happening in Israel now is that we have a development of arguments between religious and non-religious people in the context of the affairs of the Nation, and that is the problem. And this Zionist, the father of the secular Israeli soldier who attacks the religious officer, has no right to attack the officer's religious opinions. This father has a right to be an Atheist if that is what he wants. The world knows, I mean there are continuous arguments throughout cultures, humanity was in a process of development, and this issue between religion and nationality is an old subject. Arguments between Religion and State have been going on for a long time. The separation between Religion and State, or the separation between Religion and Nationality, are not problems only facing Jews. What is the problem? The problem of Religion and State is the problem of today. For example, there are theocratic nations here in the Middle East, like the Iranians, or Saudi Arabia or Egypt. In Israel we have a little bit of this argument between Religion and State. Professor Y. Leibowitz would like a separation between Religion and State (*medina*), because he disdains the State; he does not believe in a secular state. However, he does not talk about separation between Religion and Nationality (*le'om*). In my definition of the Israeli State, Israel is still a Jewish state. There is an Israeli Nation, there is a Jewish religion, and it is possible to be, in this scenario, an Israeli, a Muslim, a Christian or one of any other persuasion. There must be equal rights for all people in the Israeli Nation. In my definition you can call Israel a *Jewish state*, in the same sense as you call America a *Christian* nation, or France a *Catholic* nation, that is, that the majority of the people who live in the state understand that there is a religious influence on the nation, and that you cannot prevent that from happening. With all the separation in America, there is an influence of Christianity. There are rules that are influenced by that, for example, to celebrate Christmas is a secular rule, not a religious one. I mean, in the state of New York, everything is closed on Christmas; the secular state passes a law that shops should be closed. It could be the same thing here in Israel. Let a secular state, not the rabbinical authorities, decide that on Yom Kippur nobody works. Pay attention: not the rabbinate, but a state authority which is secular will decide. This separation gives an opportunity for people of different religions to receive equality through the law. Separation of entities, the same as in America. This difficult situation which we are now in, let's try to figure it out. Zionism was a mixture of a national movement and religion. In the last 1900 years, Jews lived as a religious nationality, and since they did not have any sovereignty it did not disturb anybody, including them. It is only after many generations, when we started talking about life in a Jewish state, a return to the Land of Israel, the leadership did not think forward, but was thinking backwards: *Hashiveinu Adonai Eloheinu l'tziyon ircha b'rachamim* – Return us G-d to Zion with mercy. And it is definitely a Return. What is missing was a political leadership that would rise and say if we want a sovereign nation, a nation of free people on its land, we must update ourselves. We cannot be a free nation like Saudi Arabia; we would like to be a free nation like France or England or America.

These issues have never been dealt with. And the proof that I am right is the fact that nobody is dealing with these issues even today. All sorts of people have said all sorts of things about me and my associates, but none has dealt with the issue of the separation of religion and nationality: Jewish religion, Israeli nationality. What is happening in Israel is that people are living in Mysticism; I'm saying what needs to happen to the Jewish people is that somebody will stop saying that they are optimistic. The Jewish people are optimistic? Six-million dead Jews is not enough? -- I am pessimistic. They say Pharaoh, Haman, Hitler: where are they?

And where are we Jews? We are in the process of dissolution!

A young student driving a taxi in New York City, an American, not Jewish, gave me a ride through mid-town Manhattan. We started talking about Israel. He said to me, "I do not understand one thing, and I am not against Jews or Israelis, but why did you have to put Israel in Palestine?" For him, an Israeli and a Jew is the same thing. I answered him that Israel is there for the same reason that France is where it is; France is a young nation, Israel is an old nation. The way things are developing today, there is confusion over the issue of the Israeli national identity, that nobody recognizes. People talk about "Israelis" and enter the word "Jews." This issue of Israeli national identity is not going to stand the test of time. Sooner or later, people will start understanding that the Jews want to have their cake and eat it too, and this will lead to troubles. In my opinion, the first ones to abandon Israel will be the Jewish Americans, not the Gentile Americans. The Jews in America are starting to ignore Israel. In the Holocaust time, the owner of the *Washington Post*, Eugene Meyer, attacked us [the Bergson Group] because the Zionists put all sorts of ideas into his head. He was an assimilated Jew, and the Zionists told him that we, the people of the Hebrew Committee of National Liberation, think that Eugene Meyer's place is not in America, that he should leave for Palestine, and it is sort of a funny thing that his wife Agnes, who is not Jewish, was part of our Emergency Committee to Save Jews in 1943.

In one way or another, Professor Wyman maybe was right that we sinned by creating the Hebrew Committee of National Liberation. But, I don't think that he is correct. If we took that step in 1943, he is right, but we did not create the Hebrew Committee of National Liberation until the creation of the War Refugee Board in 1944. According to Wyman, the War Refugee Board was our biggest achievement. But I don't think so. The WRB was a big achievement, but also a disaster. They suddenly changed the Jews to "Refugees." In Europe they were slaughtering Jews, and in Washington they were talking about refugees. We absolutely could not come out against the WRB; we were locked in a trap. In January 1944, time was of the essence, and if we were to try to attack the WRB, it would only hurt the possibility of saving some Jews. The WRB did, to a limited extent, what they could. When May 1944 arrived, we were in a desperate situation. We thought that it would be more essential to do what we were doing on the much larger and basic question of preserving the concept of Hebrew nationality. When you are talking about the massacre of a nation, that is, murdering also the soul of the nation, you are not just killing the body. And we needed to think about the future, to throw out some hope. Now, you have to look at the cruelty and craziness in which people attacked us. We knew that people would attack us – we were not that naïve, but we were hoping for an intellectual attack, about substance; that never happened.

[I asked Bergson if there is such a thing as the Jewish People-EM]

When the Hebrew Committee of National Liberation was established in May 1944 in Washington, we started talking about the "Jewish People." He said, "Of course there is a Jewish People; I do not know exactly what the meaning of "people" is, there are many definitions of this concept of people. What I am talking about is the Jewish people, the historical Jewish people, that has existed as a religious nationality instead of a religious state. When Jews lived outside of the Land of Israel, the issue of nationality was not important. One was a minister, or advisor to the Sultan, or a Prime Minister -- all the Jews were the same because they did not have any Jewish sovereignty. One was Trotsky, and the other was just a refugee. When the Israeli Nation was established in May 1948, a transitional period started, and we needed to do what we could intellectually to direct this transitional period. There was a need to discuss the revolution that happened to the Jewish people. The right for self-definition was given to Jews who wanted it, who wanted to belong to the Hebrew or Israeli nation, those who wanted to go back to Israel. Because we were living in a transitional period, it was impossible to change 1900 years of a way of living as Jews by suddenly introducing laws or constitutions. But you can establish some basic rules without immediately writing a constitution. The English, for example, many people say they don't have a constitution, but I believe they do have an historical constitution, a long period of time with a rule of law. In Israel there are a few principle basic laws, but for the real basic rules there are no written laws. When I am talking about

about fundamental, basic laws, I am referring to the Israeli political identity. Who is an Israeli? The Israeli Declaration of Independence, read by Ben Gurion, was a declaration of an administrative entity rather than the declaration of a sovereign nation, because he thought that the people of this nation are the Jewish People. He well understood that the Israeli Nation is not a nation of all the Jews; he said one thing but meant another. The Israeli Declaration of Independence is a hodge-podge of contradictory sentences, and, worse than that, those who wrote and signed this Declaration did not fulfill what the Declaration promised: how can you offer equality to all religions in a religious Jewish State? Did the Jew in any Christian nation expect equality, search for equality? In 1967, all the Western world was with us, and today most of the Western world is against us. In 1967 it was clear that the State of Israel was what everybody thought: a new democratic nation. President Carter, all the time when he spoke about Israel, called it an "Israeli Nation," and in Hebrew they were translating this "*Medinat Yisrael.*" [Due to the fact that the founders of the State did not understand Hebrew well, they called it the State of Israel rather than the Israeli Nation. In Hebrew grammar, *Medinat Yisrael* is an abstract noun which applies to a government ministry office, not an Israeli nation.] Sometimes I explode when I read this in the newspapers. By the way, the Egyptians also refer to the Israelis as an Israeli Nation. If there is no Israeli nation, all we did is work for nothing.

I am convinced that there is an Israeli Nation, but it is a nation that does not know that it exists. I define myself as an "Occupied Israeli!" I am an Israeli, and I need to define what my relationship is to "Jewish" and "Israeli." In May 1948, the Jewish religion became an international religion, and the Israeli Nation inherited the political rights of the Jewish people. What is my relationship to the Jew who is not an Israeli? What is my relationship to the Israeli who is not a Jew? These are two sides of the same problem. What is my relationship to Professor Feingold in New York who teaches Jewish history? And what is my relationship to Mustafa, who works and lives in Tel Aviv? Nobody wants to deal with that subject matter. They talk always about the West Bank but forget that we have six-hundred thousand Palestinian Arabs who live in Israel and carry Israeli identity cards.

Translated and Transcribed by Eliyho Matz.

CHAPTER THREE

THE MOST IMPORTANT JEWISH PERSON IN THE PAST 2000 YEARS: TRYING TO SAVE THE JEWS, AND THE ISRAELIS. A CONVERSATION WITH HILLEL KOOK, AKA PETER BERGSON, 1980

Looking at Jabotinsky's glasses on my bookshelf...

Most people probably think that I am a bit off the wall to suggest that Peter Bergson is the most important Jew in the past 2000 years. However, the tragedy of the Holocaust has no equal in the history of the Jews. Thus, one must look at what this man did that he deserves to be given this title. This conversation will explore that issue.

HILLEL KOOK: Our approach to the Jewish people [European Jews] was not ideological, but it was a practical approach. I was born in a Lithuanian ghetto, and I was very young when we arrived in Palestine. My meeting with Jews in the Diaspora, in Warsaw, for the first time in 1937 [Mr. Kook arrived in Warsaw as a representative of the Irgun Zvai Leumi from British Palestine], was a total astonishment and shock. Dealing with them had a humane element. These people, this girl, this young man, this family -- these people we needed to take to Palestine, the total opposite of Weizmann and his fellow Zionists [the Zionists were looking for young pioneers, *chalutzim*]. Without ideology, in the most simple way the same as the Israeli Nation is the goal, you should enter culture, morality, technology, cleanliness, etc., but the main goal was an Israeli Nation, exactly the opposite of what Professor Shlomo Avineri says [Avineri recently wrote a book about the ideologies of Zionism]. For me, what Professor Avineri says is the Jewish sickness, and not the healing of Jews. The sickness continues.

[ELIYHO: Are you an Existentialist?]

HILLEL KOOK: I hate ideologies per se, even ideologies that I agree with I hate, because ideologies distort life. Even healthy ideologies do so. Our response, and the reason we responded, the way I felt, basically because the Committee for a Jewish Army was not for the ideology of an army, or for the ideology of a nation. It was specifically for the solution of the deep, troubled issues facing East European Jewry. This was the big difference between Weizmann and Jabotinsky: Weizmann's Zionism, their beliefs, were ideology combined with mysticism. Our Zionism was pragmatic. They were dealing with one more cow and one more goat, and we dealt with politics. Jabotinsky used to say that you Zionists are saying that we are not practical people. That's not true. You [main Zionists] are more photogenic. A cow and a goat you can photograph; that does not mean that a political idea, a political thought, cannot be photographed. He [Jabotinsky] used to talk about it in his speeches. I am not a big expert about Jabotinsky. He was aware about the problem, and he was looking for solutions, and he looked for something photogenic. All this introduction is an attempt to answer your question, Eliyho, why did we go to the Congress of the United States [mid-1943]? It could have not been more natural than to go to the Congress, when the purpose was to save the Jews. We had many ideas among ourselves, and we listened to others, too. We were not going to attempt to save 1000 Jews, not that it wasn't important to save 1000 Jews, and not that we said that we aren't going to do that. But our main duty, our basic idea, was political. My brain was focusing or working on one issue: how do we convince the Americans, the British, the Russians, that because the Germans are employing military personnel in the middle of the War to exterminate Jews, those who are opposing Germany must automatically do exactly the opposite. How can you say that you couldn't do it? During the War, the Allies dealt with all sorts of issues. How do we take the issue of extermination and give it a priority? We had to emphasize that this extermination is an act of war by the Germans against the Allies, so how do we make it difficult for them to kill Jews? This is what we said to the Allies, this is a front you have to deal with. We did not speak only about the humanitarian issue. We needed to convince the Allies about their moral duty. If you are not going to fight the Germans [the German extermination of Jews], there is not much of a difference between you and the Germans – you are animals like them. We convinced many people, Harold Ickes, the Interior Secretary in the Roosevelt administration -- it is not typically accepted that members of the Cabinet were willing to join our Committee. Ickes was the honorary chairman of our Emergency Committee to Save the Jewish People of Europe [in Washington, DC]. Rabbi Wise [a renowned American Reform rabbi] wrote him a nasty letter and asked him to resign, and in the letter he said that we are terrible and irresponsible people. Ickes was a very important politician. I saw him a few times at his office; he actually invited me for a conversation. He had a lot of power. From that conversation I understood that Wise threatened him, but Ickes wrote him back and told him that he is thanking the Rabbi but he doesn't need any advice on how to handle his own affairs. The work with Ickes was easy. When I went to see him, I thought he would resign; the Gentiles responded properly. To find rabbis who would participate in a march in Washington at the end of 1943 was much more difficult than to convince a Cabinet Secretary to support the Emergency Committee to Save the Jewish People of Europe. There was an attempt to make the issue of saving European Jews an official task of the United States government, and in order to pursue that goal you needed to create public pressure, and also to find a *modus operandi*; you do that by the President of the United States creating a body that will save Jews. When the War Refugee Board was established in January 1944, we were talking about millions of dollars that were available for that task, and here those Jewish organizations started with their nonsensical approach to the problem. Our friends in the Treasury Department told us that the President had millions of dollars in hand that didn't need any Congressional approval for spending.

After 1941 we suddenly discovered America: an American Jew by the name of Alfred Strelsin. In one of the meetings we had about creating a Jewish Army, Strelsin suggested that we call the army The

Committee for a *Palestinian* Army – not a *Jewish* army. In those days I was a regular Zionist, and America was neutral. The term Jewish army was problematic. Mr. Strelsin said to me, Peter, if there will be a Jewish army, should I join it? I answered him, no, you are an American, and your place is in the American army. It sounds today very simple: there is an Israeli Nation (Jewish State) for 32 years already, and they still live in a world of dreams, as well as in a world of lies. I am talking about those ideas from the end of the 1940's. We were trying to be practical people. In 1941 we were still simple Zionists who dealt with Jews. Practically, Strelsin was a Jew. It is true that his situation was not like the Jew who lived in Poland, but for us there wasn't much difference between an American Jew and a Polish Jew, the same as Ben Gurion saw it, and today Shimon Peres and Menachem Begin see it that way. In 1941, we solved the problem in a pragmatic way, and we called it the Committee of a Jewish Army of Stateless and Palestinian Jews. The wagon came before the horse; the solution came before the question. We said that there is a big difference between a Palestinian Jew, between a Jew who is a refugee without any nationality, and between an American Jew, an English Jew and a French Jew. Who is Mr. Strelsin? Suddenly we discovered that Mr. Strelsin is a Jew, another type of a Jew; we are not two same

Jews. Mr. Strelsin is an American Jew. And because of that we started thinking, forward and back, we actually started thinking backwards. We were in the middle of the extermination and in total shock [1941]. There was an honest attempt to deal with Mr. Strelsin and myself, an intellectual honesty. We were both Jews, but there was a big difference between us. In those days I understood the confusion of identity, the confusion between reality and dream, between "Jewish people" separated and confused, one is a German Jew, the other one is a French Jew, and the third is an English Jew who shoot at each other in the battle [WWI]. This lie, this tragedy of Jewish unity there is no such thing, there is the opposite. It is the same thing today [emphasized by banging his fist on the table], this big lie about the unity of the Jewish people, between the American Jew and the Israeli Jew, and one day it will explode. Jews always lived in their own realm of reality, that was totally disconnected from reality. In reality, they lived within the grace of the Gentiles. The Gentiles killed us and gave us all sorts of troubles, but they also provided us with water and a place to sleep. Therefore, Jews as a nation have absolutely no concept of practical politics.

For 1900 years they did not deal with practical issues. For example, take Mr. [Menachem] Begin – he reminds me of the old Jewish story about the Jew in the shtetl who returns home after a gang of Gentiles beats him up and tells his wife what happened, and she in response says, 'and you didn't say anything to them?' The classical difference between talking and doing does not exist between Jews. In all the activities of the Israeli Nation, after 100 years of Zionism, there is a difference between a submachine gun and political thought. All throughout the years of Zionism, the leadership did not emphasize that Zionism is a national liberation movement for sovereignty for those who have no choice or those who make the choice; those who wish otherwise should do otherwise. Zionism always spoke about unity among Jews. When I arrived in America in 1940, I understood that there is an American Jew and a Polish Jew, but the twist in my head happened during the Holocaust; I realized that there are major problems here. I wrote a long letter in 1944 to Weizmann about it. Mr. Strelsin, who first raised the question about his identity, did not really know what he was saying, but in essence he was right. I arrived back in Israel on the 16th of May [1948] because I made a promise to Rabbi Wise during the Holocaust. In those days we tried to save European Jews, and we had a meeting with Dr. Wise, and Dr. Wise yelled at us and said that in Palestine there are 500,000 Jews, and here in America our group activities [the

Bergson Group] is endangering five-million Jews. It was difficult for me to understand him. And then in 1943 when we presented in Congress the idea of saving Jews, the Zionists and Rabbi Wise came out against us. You know, those rabbis used to yell; they had sort of a Shakespearean voice, and Wise was yelling, 'In whose name are you speaking?' So I said to him, 'Do you want me to go to the death camps in Europe and conduct elections there? We are acting according to our conscience as a Hebrew nation [in May 1944 Bergson opened a Hebrew Embassy in Washington, DC]. We feel responsibility that we have to save our people, and we are sorry that we are doing very little with all our yelling. And you, Rabbi Wise, say that we are yelling too much, because you are an American and I am a Hebrew and both of us are Jews. You are from a Hebrew origin [as he bangs his fist repeatedly on the desk], and I am a Hebrew today, and as soon as a small piece of the Hebrew nation [Palestine] will be sovereign, I will be there. And you will continue to be an American clergyman of the Jewish faith and a member of the Democrat party, and Rabbi Silver, your colleague, will remain here as an American clergyman and will be a member of the Republican party, and after I said all those things hundreds of times I traveled to Israel on the fifteenth of May 1948 but arrived on the sixteenth.

In 1943, when we tried to pass legislation about saving the Jews of Europe, and Wise came out against us, I had an argument with Wise, and I tried to explain to him that what he was doing was wrong. I gave him the example, an imaginary situation in which we now sit and discuss things and suddenly there is a fire in the building. As a young man, I will run out and start yelling, 'Please save Rabbi Wise, he is inside.' But according to your politics, Rabbi Wise, you want me to say, 'There is a fire in the building, please reserve a room for Rabbi Wise in the Waldorf Astoria.' Because according to you, Rabbi Wise, you are saying, 'Save the Jews by bringing them to Palestine.' But to mention Palestine today in the Congressional resolution is a terrible mistake, because as a political issue it will not resolve anything. Opening the gates of Palestine is mysticism, it's an ideology that is not realistic in the middle of the War. It's like Soviet ideology today [1980], you are trying to free the working class, and the working class becomes slaves. You are trying to save the Jewish human being, and after thirty-two years we have again a ghetto here [in Israel]. And because they have a flag and an army, it means nothing. When the War Refugee Board was established in 1944, we won, but in reality we were defeated. The War Refugee Board was a recognition of the fact that we had political power, but our real goal of saving Jews was not accepted, because Hitler did not kill refugees.

Translated & Transcribed by Eliyho Matz.

CHAPTER FOUR

ISRAELI TRACTATUS – UN LOGICO "NOBODY WANTS TO TALK ABOUT IT" IT'S 1776 IN PALESTINE

The following conversation with Hillel Kook, a.k.a. Peter Bergson, took place in 1980 in Manhattan, New York City. I am trying to present his words more or less as I understood them.

HILLEL KOOK: I am talking about identity…the State of Israel, the way she is, her purpose is not to be concerned about the welfare of its citizens or their wellbeing. That's how a person [Arik Sharon] can walk around and declare that we are going to be in a war for the next two-hundred years…not in any other nation…in another place they would have thrown him to hell if he dared to speak to people and tell them that we are planning to be at war for the next two-hundred years. Since in Israel there is no Israeli nationality (*leom yisraeli*), this is an ideology and beside it a lie…You scratch a young Israeli, he is an anti-Semite to a certain degree, to a certain degree with justice because he feels in one way or another that something in the history is not okay, and he cannot figure it out. In my opinion, after 32 years there is simply no basic discussion.

I tried to explain this to people in New York, nobody listens. What is my relationship as a human being, as an Israeli, as a Jew, to an Israeli who is not Jewish, or an Israeli Arab, or a Muslim Palestinian? [Hillel does not imply the demeaning use of the word "Arab," which is common among Jewish Israelis. He sees Arabic as a language and a culture. What he does not intend is the Israeli expression that is shallow, and politically and socially irresponsible toward the Palestinians.] And what is your relationship [Eliyho] to a Jew who is not an Israeli? Here there is a triangle: Kissinger, Sheik Abu Rabia [Bedouin member of the Israeli Knesset], and [Menachem] Begin. If you take seriously the decision of the Israeli Supreme Court that says that an Israeli, a Hebrew and a Jew are the same thing, what comes out of that is that the Sheik Abu Rabia is a Jew, and Kissinger is an Israeli; I think that Judge Olshen ruled on that issue. I think, I am saying, that this abnormal Jewish existence is not really that important insofar as it created Nobel Prize winners and many other good things. I thought and I think that the Jews are a mix from an historical point of view [I mentioned to Hillel the issue of conversion that nobody talks about as an historical force in Judaism--EM]. Judaism is not something unique. Every tribe and nation, all the tribes, had a G-d, and they also had a connection to a territory...our preservation is the unique thing about us.

We remained and survived and meanwhile all the development and progress of human civilization and culture jumped up on us.

In reality, the separation between religion and nationality was a process that started a few hundred years ago, and in reality is not finished. In Saudi Arabia they don't know what it means. But in Europe they know what it means. This jumped up on us. When I grew up, there were millions of Jews who wanted to leave the lands, the countries, which they lived in; they didn't have where to go. If the gates of America were not closed [American immigration laws changed in the 1920's to prevent Jews from coming to America], there would not be an Israeli State [Hillel means the Israeli Nation that was born in 1948; its name *Medinat Yisrael* is an abstract noun that is actually defined as "a government ministry"]. If American immigration laws did not change in the 1920's, lots of European Jews would have come to America. This would have released the pressure in Europe and probably would have helped Jews in Europe.

We [the Bergson Group] fought from 1940 to 1948 in America for the right of self-determination. Zionists today, like Professor Avineri, claim today that Zionism was a national liberation movement of the Jewish people, and I say that the Jewish people today is not subjugated and also does not exist as an entity, and therefore cannot fight as an entity. It's like the story of a crazy man in a room, the door is open, and he can go out, but he's not going out. How can you say that somebody is a freedom fighter? Those who are enclosed in a room can fight for freedom -- they are closed in and they are fighting for freedom. We fought [through broad political activities in the US]. When we won, we didn't come to the right conclusions and we didn't change the structure of the Nation. It's impossible that you want to be a nation, you want to be strong, you want to be sovereign, and at the same time you want to be a persecuted refugee, also crying, everything together. There is a basic, simple issue: separation between religion and nationality [*dat v'leom*, not like in Israel where leaders drive people crazy talking about religion and state, *dat u'medinah*]. The separation between religion and nationality, first of all for the simple reason of religion. Israel is destroying the religion; you must separate between religion and nationality [*dat v'leom*]. On this subject they don't want to talk. Once I spoke to a group of American Jewish professors who live in Israel and in America. I blamed them that they took away the country from me. I fought all my adult life for freedom, and I am finding myself now living in a Jewish ghetto. I am living in a Jewish ghetto because you Americans do not want to give up your America! If you give me America, I will agree that Israel will be a Jewish state. You took away from the Israelis their national identity! You don't recognize the Israeli Nation; according to you there is no Israeli Nation, and therefore Israel will be destroyed, from the inside and the outside. Nobody is forcing you to live in the *Galut*, the diaspora. There is no *galut* after 1948; the *galut* is over. But, the theological *galut* continues. Even those who live in Jerusalem today are in a theological *galut*. The Messiah did not arrive. Begin and Rabin are not the *Moshiach's* [Messiah's] messengers. On this issue I am in total agreement with the [ultra-Orthodox] group Neturei Karta, and this confusion created something which is not a people, not a nation, and not a religion. Rabbi Goren is not a rabbi, he is a Catholic bishop. I studied together with him at the yeshiva; it's not Judaism. A Chief Rabbi that is elected by the Knesset is not a Chief Rabbi – he is a *smartut* [dishrag], he is a government clerk. A Jew who respects the Jewish religion needs to have contempt for him. A rabbi is something that I choose: they say in the Talmud, "Make yourself a rabbi."

The separation between religion and nationality: the recognition of the renewal of part of the Land of Israel, the Hebrew Israeli Nation -- for me "Hebrew" expresses a better historical understanding, "Hebrew" is closer to nationality. You celebrate the holiday of *Pesach* [Passover] – it's a national and religious holiday combined together. But all right, let it be an Israeli [holiday], there is an Israeli Nation, and you have to make a decision. Do we want to be a nation like Saudi Arabia, or like an Iranian nation, or a modern nation? You can make many speeches about the fact that we are a modern nation, but in reality we are a Theocracy. The birth of the Israeli Nation made Judaism a universal religion, like Christianity. You have to get used to the idea that there are many good Jews like the Lubavicher rabbi, or the Chief Rabbi of Brazil, or the rabbi of Communist Rumania, that they are good Jews and are equal to the Jews in Israel from the point of view of religion. Israel is one of the countries of the world from the point of view of a modern nation that has Jews. Israel is different a bit because it's the only nation in the world where the majority of its inhabitants are Jews. Apropos, not all of them are Jews, and therefore the majority will choose, like in America, if a bank will be closed on Yom Kippur. From the point of view of religion, the Israeli Nation, as long as its inhabitants will want, will be a Jewish state, the same as America is a Christian nation. You cannot say that America is not a Christian nation, even though it's not called the United States of Christian America. The most critical thing is the separation between religion and nationality, an option for those who are not Jews who would like to be citizens, Israeli citizens, Israeli nationals. I am not saying that we are going to open the gates of the nation and will flood it with 30-million Japanese. I do not like those intellectuals like Avineri who say that Israel cannot just be a regular nation like Belgium. Israel is Belgium. If we are going to introduce intellectual context to the Israeli Nation, it will be better than Belgium; today it is worse than Belgium. In Israel now there is one issue that, because of Israeli clumsiness, has become an international issue. The settlements on the West Bank are a combination of a religious disgrace and an Israeli national security disgrace. These people from Gush Emunim -- my cousin is their leader but he is an old useless man. When the Holy Ari [a Kabbalistic thinker] lived in Safed, did he try to overturn the Turkish authorities? Did it bother him that there was Turkish rule? He would probably have been very happy if there was a Judaic kingdom, but that is not why he lived there. Jews have lived in Jerusalem for many generations; if you want to live in the West Bank in the town of Shilo, go and live there, but if you want to use and abuse Judaism to conquer a piece of land because of politics, that's a completely different story. You cannot discern a difference between Arik Sharon the Atheist, and Rabbi Levinger the Clericalist; everything is total confusion.

    About Israel and Zionism, there are probably 5000 books written. Not a single one is about our [the Bergson Group's] work in the United States. We raised questions from 1940 till 1948, and we succeeded in creating a debate. If we didn't raise these questions on Hebrew nationality, I'm doubtful that the Israeli Nation would have been established when it was established. We succeeded, mostly among non-Jews (Netanyahu's father was against us). We succeeded in explaining to non-Jews what Zionism is. Zionism was a national liberation movement. We fought for a free Palestine: IT'S 1776 IN PALESTINE! The year 1776 -- in America everyone knows and understands what 1776 means. In Israel today it sounds like I'm trying to teach the Zohar [Kabbalah]. All the problems stem from the fact that there was never a political basis for the Israeli Nation. If you want to be sovereign and free, you need to express it. In Israel, we use the word *medinah* [state] instead of *leom* [nation]. What is a *medinah*, what kind of value is expressed in the word *medinah*? *Medinah* is an instrument of the people. If we had some basic laws that would define the Israeli nationality, we could have resolved the issue of the non-Jews living in Israel. We have 700-thousand Palestinians whom we call by mistake "Arabs"; if you would have given them political equality, this would have changed the Israeli nation from the inside. To those Palestinians who do not want to participate in becoming Israeli nationals, you can say that you can be residents here as long as you obey the laws. All concepts and lies between Jews and Arabs -- if we could have resolved the issues between Israelis and Palestinians residing in Israel, we would be able to reach peace with the surrounding nations. Today instead, we are a dual-national nation. Let's not talk about solutions, let's talk about a conversation. Isn't it suspicious to you, Eliyho, that there was no conversation, and you didn't hear about it when you grew up in Rishon Lezion? I argue that the nation of Israel, that the way it exists today, from a point of view of basic political issues, the nation has developed this way one-hundred percent because people did not have any intellectual concept, or, as Ben Gurion expressed it, "*partza hamedinah*," the nation has erupted.

The concept of nationality was an improvisation: they took the totality of Jewish history and added to it a *medinah*, a state. The Jews lived in the *Galut* [Diaspora] for hundreds of years. The time had come and a new nation, an independent Jewish nation, was established. A call was made to all Jews, the Law of Return -- come to settle here -- and after 32 years they still talk about the *Galut*. Nobody paid attention that there is a basic difference between the fact that the Lubavicher rebbe, when he was in Russia and prayed about the Land of Israel, could not actually leave Russia because they did not let him out, and here today the Lubavicher rebbe that sits in New York, and his Chassidim, happily get into an El Al plane to travel to Israel, return to New York, and say that they are in the *Galut*. It's okay to talk about a theological *galut*; the messiah has not arrived. But they call *Medinat Yisrael "atchalta d'geulah,"* the "beginning of salvation." About *galut*, even atheists that don't believe in G-d speak about it. The Jewish people have no concept of what sovereignty is. They talk about *medinah* [state], not about a nation. *Medinah* [state] is an instrument of the people. It's all confused because they did not free the human being. I feel like a liberated Jew: I am an Israeli because I want to be an Israeli. But there is no definition in the law: Israel, the nation of Israelis, is not really so. They took the Jewish uniqueness, the good and the bad, the negative and the positive, and confused them. Jewish uniqueness was not because of choice. A small part did not want to be Jewish; a big part remained Jewish. Some of those who remained Jewish lived in a ghetto, and part of the Jews lived among many other nations in different statuses of equality or inequality. Zionism was supposed to solve the physical problem of Jews who did not want to stay in Eastern Europe. The Israeli Nation today avoids looking at the major event that happened to the Jews who were needing to be saved during the Holocaust but were exterminated instead. Zionism was a political movement to solve the problems of people that had a physical need to be saved, the same as they hungry Irish who came on boats to America at the time of the big hunger. Israel has no foundations because nobody sat down to plan and connect between realism and mysticism. Zionism remained an ideological movement, disconnected from any reality, that creates its own reality -- like the Communism in Russia that was supposed to free man but made him a slave.

I am an Israeli, I am a Jew, a resident of Israel -- the word "Israeli" is a total lie....For example, Mohammed in Jaffa, in Yaffo, in this dirty ghetto where he lives, where they didn't pave a road for 32 years, it doesn't disturb all the liberals who write articles while sitting in a restaurant just outside this ghetto, thirty meters from this dirty slum. Nobody has done anything practical, and this Mohammed is an Israeli citizen the same as I am. Nobody pays attention that in the Israeli nation there is no definition of an Israeli nationality. In the Israeli Declaration of Independence, Ben Gurion promised elections and a Constitutional Assembly that would write a constitution that would promise equal rights for all citizens despite religious differences. So they came to the Arab villages that lived under military rule, a pretty severe military rule because there was a war, and they told them you are becoming Israeli citizens, and they gave them Israeli identity cards. They did not say to them, you have an option if you want to become a Israeli citizen, and if you want to be one you are obligated to some sort of loyalty. They came to people who were conquered and made them citizens. In 1966 I spoke to Ben Gurion and I asked him if there was any place in Israel where three people sat down together to figure out the complicated issue of nationality; there was never such a thing. In the Constitutional Assembly I suggested a law that Israel should have one language -- they threw that suggestion into *pach hazevel*, the garbage pail. What remained is what we had under British rule, that Arabic is an official language: from a practical point of view, everyone knows how official it is. The relationship to the Jews who live outside Israel -- there is no serious conversation about it. The mere existence of Israel tells you that it's not like a normal state, like an administrative instrument of its own people. We are trying to internalize without much thinking the abnormal dispersion that was forced on us for 2000 years: supposedly we were freed, but I say that the individual is not free. I define myself as an Israeli, I am an Israeli and I want to be an Israeli. In Europe, there was a concept developed between nationality and citizenship. To Americans it is very difficult to explain the difference between citizenship and nationality. In the Knesset I voted for the Law of Return. I didn't conceive that they were going to make from it, or equate it with, the Ten Commandments. From a point of view of national identity, I am a Jew, a resident of Israel, and Kissinger is a Jew, a resident of America.

This is the Israeli situation.

Translated and Transcribed by Eliyho Matz.

CHAPTER FIVE

CONCURRENT RESOLUTION: A WAR IN THE AMERICAN CONGRESS, 1943 THE GENTILES TRY TO SAVE JEWS, THE JEWS TRY TO PREVENT THEIR DOING SO

[For a comprehensive look at this Concurrent Resolution to save Jews during the Holocaust, see Chapter 11, "The Rescue Resolution," in David S. Wyman's book *The Abandonment of the Jews*.]

HILLEL KOOK: What happened...the resolution in the United States Congress in 1943 to create a US government agency to save the Jewish people of Europe -- the emphasis is the *Jewish* people -- the emphasis was very significant even then in the beginning when we dedicated 100-percent of our energy to the rescue of Jews. We were aware that the Nazis are not killing single Jews, but a people....The resolution to save Jews was presented in both Houses of Congress; it was a Concurrent Resolution, not a regular bill, it is a type of resolution that both Houses of Congress pass, it is sort of a request presented by both bodies that usually the President cannot ignore:

it's not like a proposal for a law, but it presents a moral issue more than a regular law because it passes or proceeds on issues that are not controversial -- it passes unanimously, it is a Congressional demonstration of good will.

I was in Washington, responsible for the political work of the Emergency Committee to Save the Jewish People of Europe. Our work centered around the Congress. We did not concentrate on the State Department -- there were actually two meetings with the Secretary of State Cordell Hull. The value of these meetings came in the fact that he received us: he received a delegation of the Emergency Committee to Save the Jewish People of Europe. In July, 1943, there was in New York City an Emergency Conference that presented the State Department with proposals, and only because one of the officials at the State Department prevented the proposals from being heard -- he tried to torpedo them, some things that Hull had agreed on, for example a small delegation that would go to Turkey to try to rescue Jews from there. Breckenridge Long was the obstructing official, he really gave us a hard time, so we went to see Hull again to complain. Our strength was in the fact that twice Hull saw a delegation of ours. Hull was an old man, very respected and respectful. Our main strength was with Congressmen and Senators who were participants in the Emergency Committee to Save the Jewish People of Europe; these Congressmen and Senators arranged meetings for us. The Concurrent Resolution was before the Senate and the House. We never thought for a moment that we would have difficulties with this type of a resolution. And you know, as always, the trouble came from the most unexpected of places: the Zionists tried to convince Sol Bloom from New York, a Jewish Congressman who was the head of the House Foreign Affairs Committee, to delay the issue. His reason was that we had decided not to include Palestine as a haven in the resolution, because we knew that the mere mention of Palestine was a minefield. This type of a Concurrent Resolution was supposed to go to a committee; every such resolution needs to pass a committee, but it's not the type of a resolution that a committee holds a hearing for. It is a declaration of a humanitarian need: we are talking about thousands of Jews being murdered every day. And this Jew, Sol Bloom, influenced by Jewish Zionists, simply sat on it with all sort of excuses and evasion.

[Representative Sol Bloom, in my opinion the most despicable Jew in the history of the United States, carried out all tricks possible to prevent the Rescue resolution. Part of his tricks included conducting hearings in which he insulted and embarrassed Peter Bergson unnecessarily. Let's not forget that Peter Bergson was the main person in the United States behind the attempts to save European Jewry. To make the situation more complicated, Sol Bloom made the hearings "Executive," and therefore it took more than 30 years for them to be located, this along with the fact that the Congressional archivist who ultimately published them titled them incorrectly. Finally, I found the minutes of the

hearings after many years of research; if not by chance and obsession, I might never have found the papers. The drama disclosed in the records of the hearings reads like a Shakespearean play. – EM]

When we finally understood what the issue was, we understood that we were losing time and we despaired. We lost hope that the House would pass the resolution, so we talked to our friends in the Senate: Senator Guy Gillette from Iowa, Senator Elbert Thomas from Utah, Senator Edwin Johnson from Colorado, and other Senators who were on our Committee to save European Jews. Sol Bloom would not pass the resolution along to a committee in the House -- go and explain to a Mormon Senator from Utah whose religious conscience burdens him, that a Reform rabbi, a Zionist, does not let Sol Bloom pass such a resolution. Elbert Thomas from Utah said to me, "I will go and talk to Sol Bloom," and I told him not to waste his time. I told him he is a Congressman from New York, not from Utah. Elbert Thomas was Number Two in the Senate Committee on Foreign Relations. When he finally understood the situation, he said to me, "I will pass it in the Senate, I will not wait for the House." The Committee chairman in the Senate was a Senator from Texas, Senator Thomas Connally. The State Department told him to ignore, not to touch the resolution the same way that Rabbi Wise told Sol Bloom -- or it is possible that the State Department told Sol Bloom. Senator Thomas told me when Connally the Chairman does not come in one day, he will be sick or something, I usually take over as Number Two and I become the Chairman, and then I will pass it. In the meantime I will lobby with the Senators; I know who will agree, and those who are not sure, I'll work to convince them. Senator Thomas worked very hard with us. There were three Senators who were involved with us and very convinced on this subject of saving Jews. I mentioned them before; they worked with us every day. I don't mean that I saw them every day. I only spoke about three Senators, and I don't mean to hurt others who were involved, but these three were emotionally involved. Senator Thomas was a Mormon missionary; his wife and daughter also worked with us. Until today I cannot understand one thing: what the Jews call in jargon *Goyim*, Gentiles, they question that a Gentile would be interested in saving Jews -- and for me it's hard to understand that a Gentile would *not* be interested in saving Jews, and I come from a ghetto and they were born in America. There were all sorts of Americans, non-Jews, who had to fight with Jews in order to stay on the Emergency Committee to Save the Jewish People -- Jews who attacked and confused them.

[In a letter dated August 1, 1944, that Senator Guy Gillette, a member of the Committee on Foreign Relations, sent to Harry Louis Selden, a supporter of Hillel, Gillette wrote that "...sometime after the Resolution was introduced...Dr. Wise called at my office accompanied by two or three other gentlemen and discussed the pending Resolution with me. None of these gentlemen seemed to be enthusiastic for the passage of the Resolution and

the tenor of the conversation seemed to suggest their belief that the action as proposed by the Resolution was not a wise step to take, although they professed very strong interest in everything that would look to the saving of the remnant of the Jewish people in Europe from destruction."]

Did I ever tell you the story about Andy, Congressman Andrew Sommers? He was the first Congressman that brought up to Congress our proposal for the creation of a Jewish Army in 1940 before we created the Emergency Committee to Save the Jewish People. He was of Irish descent. He worked like one of us. He was a head of a committee in Congress; his office was my office when I used to come to the Capitol Building. He did all sorts of things for us. He had a district manager in Brooklyn, a Jew, the Democratic boss, and that boss gave him an ultimatum to resign from the Emergency Committee to Save the Jewish People. He threatened him that if he would not do so, he will not be renominated to become a Congressman, that he would choose someone else. The district in Brooklyn was mostly Democratic; in the primaries the public hardly participated. There were Jews and Irish and both were Democrats. He was as gray as a sack when he told me about the threats. I told him: please resign from our Committee. He thanked me. I told him: you are important to us as a friend, as a member of Congress. He said he would think about it. We spoke in Washington; he left for New York and came back, so I called him and I went to see him. I asked him, "Did you resign from the Emergency Committee to Save the Jewish People?" He told me quietly but bluntly that he told the district manager to go to hell (he used a dirty word). He continued, "I am a member of Congress for 20 years -- what do I know of what else I can do? The work with you guys is the most important work I have done in my life. And I know, Peter, that you are generous and you asked me to resign from the Emergency Committee to Save the Jewish People. I am not resigning." He told me that he already knows who is going to replace him, some Jewish professor. "I said to the Jewish Democratic boss in Brooklyn, 'I am a Catholic. Do you want me to resign in the middle of the massacre of Jews?' I told him to go to hell." Eventually I convinced Andy Sommers to run in the primaries. We organized a campaign for him and he won with a big majority. We in the Bergson Group were sure, we spoke about it among ourselves: why would the Irish vote for someone else, when they already voted for him ten times? We went to talk to the Jewish members of that community with that certain rabbi, and we convinced them, because Jews love a Gentile who is more radical than they are, because they were frightened; and so it was he was reelected. When I was arrested at the time of the Altalena incident in 1948, he flew to Israel to save me....

But let's continue with the Concurrent Resolution. Senator Thomas called me one day and told me the resolution passed in the Senate Foreign Relations Committee unanimously -- it took five minutes. And then the pressure started on Roosevelt. Thomas was pressuring the Democratic Majority

Leader of the Senate, Mr. Alben Barkley [Barkley later became the Vice President of the US under President Truman], even though nothing happened in the House. It was a humanitarian issue; people were being killed and murdered every day. Thomas prepared the Senate for a vote and Roosevelt didn't want the Senate to vote on it. So he created the War Refugee Board in January 1944.

Translated and transcribed by Eliyho Matz.

CHAPTER SIX

CONGRESSMAN WILL ROGERS, JR., A DESCENDANT OF NATIVE AMERICAN INDIANS, ATTEMPTS TO SAVE JEWS

[DOCUMENT]

STATEMENT FROM: Hon. Will Rogers, Jr. on the occasion of the second edition of <u>Years of Wrath – Days of Glory</u> by Yitshak Ben-Ami, former Irgun emissary and member of the Hebrew Committee for National Liberation, 1944-1948

SENT TO: Paul O'Dwyer at the Princeton Club, Wednesday, April 27, 1983

    I regret not being with you on this occasion of the Second Coming of Mike Ben-Ami's book. This is a chronicle [of] transcending importance because it is a first-hand testimony from a witness of what went on before, during, and after <u>Years of Wrath</u>. It is a story that needs telling: it is the best evidence as it dispels the mythology that is being circulated to cover up the embarrassing truth – that the Holocaust could not have been without the indifference of the Allied governments and the passive role of the Jewish establishment.

For the past several weeks, public attention has been directed at the Holocaust -- an impressive Holocaust Museum is being established in the Capital in the shadow of the Washington Monument. We are told that this is to remind us of the crime that was committed by the Nazis against defenseless people -- mostly Jews. I am not clear exactly what the meaning is of such a museum. A memorial has a place. But does it tell the story? Does it tell how the British locked the escape route, that the American government was silent, that the Jewish establishment hid, that our State Department refused visas and turned refugee boats back to Hitler's inferno? The killing was only the final act in the vast conspiracy of cruelty, indifference, and silence. The victims heard the silence. Also, Hitler heard the silence and saw that for this, for killing Jews, there was no protest, no objection.

Of course, there is the other story, Mike Ben Ami's story. The story of vision, of resistance, of courage. Amid the horror there is the story of those young men and women of Palestine and Europe who saw the writing on the wall, and warned what was coming. As early as 1939, they banded together to find boats, even build rafts, to float people down the Danube to ports where they could charter ships, and some made it through the British blockade. When the war started, they fought the Nazis, joining the British, French, Poles. Mike joined the American Army.

Above all, they also cried out against the crime that was going on. They were impolite because they were frantic. They broke the rules of etiquette, they ran full page ads telling what was happening, they broke the conspiracy of silence.

Thank God! I was one who heard their cry, and being in Congress, was able to act in a limited way. That's how I met Ben-Ami, and Peter Bergson, Sam Merlin, and the other leaders of the Hebrew Committee of National Liberation. With Senator Guy Gillette, we finally passed the resolution creating the War Refugee Board – the only action taken by the American government that actually helped save lives.

It was late in the day and only tattered fragments remained of what had been the great and talented community of 7 million European Jews (exclusive of Russia). But I remember, even then, in 1944, Sol Bloom, the chairman of the House Foreign Affairs Committee, tried to block us, and we had to go around this vain old man who was more concerned with pleasing the State Department than stopping murder.

The Holocaust is a story of the human being destroyed by his own innocence, obtuseness, self-deception – multiplied by 6 million. It is the triumph of death.

Ben-Ami's book is the little-known chronicle of how ingenuity, self-awareness, and realism can prevail. It is the triumph of life.

Please include me in any program that brings this message of realism before the widest possible audience.

>Santos Ranch
>Tubac, Arizona

CHAPTER SEVEN

ISRAEL, AMERICA, THE IRGUN TZVAI LEUMI AND THE ALTALENA FIASCO: A CONVERSATION WITH HILLEL KOOK – 1980, NEW YORK CITY

HILLEL KOOK: There is a big lie: the fact that they [Americans] said they didn't know about the Holocaust [in 1943]. How can one say that they didn't know, after we published full-page ads in major newspapers? After the rabbis' March on Washington in October, 1943, everybody knew. Hearst published an editorial on the front page of the *Journal*. Still they say today that they didn't know. Today everybody talks about Auschwitz as if, had they [the Allies] bombed Auschwitz, they would have saved all the Jews. The truth of the matter is that there was a need to do hundreds of things in attempting to save Jews. We suggested at one point to attack the Germans with poison gas; the Americans refused to do so. We are living forty years after the event, and hundreds of Jews deal with the Holocaust from Eli Wiesel up and down. My uncle, Rabbi A.H. Kook -- I used to go on the Sabbath to listen to his talks in the afternoon in Jerusalem; he always spoke on the Sabbath in the afternoon. There was one subject that he used to talk about a lot. I did not really understand him. The subject was *ahavat Yisrael*, the love of Jews. He used to repeat it -- *ahavat Yisrael, ahavat Yisrael* -- all sorts of variations on the subject. Later when I visited Israel, I spoke to one of my cousins about it. I asked him if he could explain to me these talks about *ahavat Yisrael*, and as I was asking I realized that I actually had the answer: if you don't like these people [Jews], you cannot live here in Israel. My relative answered me by saying, "You might wonder, not that this was all his intention, but he spoke about it for the purpose of rousing good relations among the Jews, so people can develop a feeling for loving Jews, for the simple reason that we can be able to live together." He did not speak about it in a cynical way, but in a constructive way.

Let me return to days of the Holocaust, and I am trying to hold down my hands and chew my fingernails in order not to become an anti-Semite. This nonsensical talk about Jewish unity: there was a conflict among Jews who lived in the Western world; the Jews were shooting at each other -- take WWI -- and while doing so they spoke about Jewish unity. We are united in our religion [only]. We speak today about unity: this rhetoric is extremely dangerous. There is a conflict, there is a potential conflict. This conflict has existed since May, 1948, and will exist as long as we do not define our Israeli nationality. Not always are the interests of Rabbi Schindler, the American Reform rabbi who headed many Jewish organizations, and Israeli interests the same. There is a need for us not to be enemies, but if we are trying to trick ourselves into some false belief of unity with full knowledge, consciously or subconsciously, that this can't be so, we are going to do damage as if we are enemies. The American Jewish leadership is convincing the American people that the United States involvement in the Middle East is because of Jews -- this is terrible. You create a collision, because we are refusing to recognize the fact that there are legitimate differences: you cannot ask an American Jew to behave as if he lives in Atlit or Haifa. The structure is sick. Leaders on both sides are cheating each other so they can get an emotional kick, a reward without a payment, and conflict will erupt. I do not believe in the basic thesis of the *mitbolelim*, the assimilated, those who said before the creation of the Israeli nation that the sheer existence of Israel would be bad for Jews. What I am saying is, the way Israel is structured will bring tragedy to Israel and to Jews because it is based on lies and unreality, because Israelis say that Israel belongs to what they call the Jewish People [*Ha'am HaYehudi*]. They say that Kissinger is not an American [but rather a Jew], and somehow somebody will get the idea. When you go to Hebron you can go to Hebron like the Holy Ari went to Safad, but when you go to Hebron in the name of religion and you exploit religion for a political purpose....

    Jews in this country, in America, feel insecure when they talk about Israel; total confusion. In 1944, the Hebrew Committee for National Liberation in the United States translated mystical Zionism to a language human beings can understand, so that every Gentile could understand us: a nation, a people, of Hebrews, that want to live independently; with the basic right for self-definition like all other nations; and like all other nations, religion is a separate issue. This Israeli Nation is not for American Jews -- the American Jews don't need it; it's not for Brazilian Jews. It is for Jews who need it, Jews who cannot or are unable to connect or don't want to be connected to nations who reject them. Who will ever think that Jews will choose to return to Germany, that burned them? The Americans understood it, American Jews understood it, even the State Department understood it: when Americans talk about Jews they think about Jews that they know, they don't think about Jews in Timbuktu. The Israeli Nation received the admiration of the world because the Western world did not understand what the Zionists were talking about. They understood Israel the way we explained it, the way it should have been. What happened in *Medinat Yisrael* is not Hillel or Eliyho: the term *Medinat Yisrael* is an abstract noun, it is best defined to mean a government office....

The Etzel Irgun Tzvai Leumi split in the 1940's, and the Lechi Lochamei Herut Yisrael started taking action [in Palestine]; the Etzel [in Palestine] did not. Because of the War, we [the Bergson Group in America] had very little contact with Palestine. We tried to do something; we worked for the creation of a Jewish Army. Do you think the Etzel in Jerusalem had any discussions about what to do when the Germans started exterminating Jews? There were no such discussions. We in America saw what was a national duty to a people who call themselves Etzel. When the situation became severe, the English did not change their policy. We did not call to save the Jews by bringing them to Palestine, because we knew it would only harm the situation. On the other hand, there was a need to change the policy in Palestine, so we sent one of our guys, Arieh Ben Eliezer, to Palestine in 1943. When Ben Eliezer arrived in Palestine, he reorganized the Etzel and he chose Menachem Begin to be their commander. This was done with my understanding and agreement; unless I agreed to that, it would not have happened. Begin, later on it was discovered, was a big problem. I was in Washington eight years and never contacted the virus of a politician, but he [Begin] who led a violent national liberation movement, he was the violent part of it; he was among people who took up arms and explosives, and he decided to be a politician: this is betrayal. I am reading in the newspaper *Ha'aretz* that he met with the old members of the Etzel and they sang the hymn of Beitar [the Revisionists], what is he *haking in chinik*? Did Dov Gruner [an Irgun member who was hanged by the British] die because he fought for a party? Did they hang him as a Revisionist, or as a freedom fighter for the Israeli Nation? I am not saying that a party cannot create an underground, but did I do what I did for a political party?

He called me ... "he" meaning I. Ben Ami ...a few months ago...called me suddenly and told me that he is writing a memoir, a book, and so on and so forth. Then he asked me, when you, Hillel, flew with Alex Hadany to Israel in 1948, how long did you stay? I answered him, "for a week," so he asked how it was possible that I stayed for a week and did not make an effort to see Menachem Begin. "Itzchaq," I answered, "where have you been?" Alex left after three days and I stayed for a week, and Alex wrote a memo about it in which he tells how we met with Begin on the first day we arrived in Israel, that we sat all night in Gidi Palgin's apartment. This Itzchaq was confused. He asked me how come they didn't write about it in the history books? So I asked him, "Do you want those liars to write about this event?" Begin hardly writes about the Hebrew Committee of National Liberation in his book *The Mered, The Revolt*. That night in May, 1948, we sat in Gidi's apartment: Hadani, Rafaeli, Landau, Meridor and a few others. It was after Begin had given a speech on the radio. Hadany suggested to Begin that he should take me, Hillel, the next time he goes to see Ben Gurion. Begin responded, "What are you talking about? What meeting? I am not going to meet that *boged* [betrayer]." I entered into the conversation by saying to Begin, "You mean to say that you did not meet him?" And Begin responded, "With this collaborator with the British, with this criminal, you want me to meet?" I said to him, "I heard you say a blessing in the name of the Israeli Nation, *beshem hamalechut* – are you saying you do not recognize the Government? Do you recognize the Government? And what will happen with the Etzel? Begin responded that the Etzel will continue to fight in Jerusalem, they will continue to fight for the entire land of Israel. Ben Gurion doesn't ask for Jerusalem. So I answered him, "How long do you think this fighting will continue in Jerusalem? One thing or the other -- either we will win or the Arabs will win. How can you continue with the Etzel in

Jerusalem? Ben Gurion will have to find some formula." This conversation took place after Israel's Declaration of Independence. Begin was not stupid, but he was not a statesman: he was an *askan*, a political *apparatchik*, and I did not understand that exactly at the time. What he did and said was that he needed to satisfy the extremists Eli Tavin, Shmuel Merlin and Aryeh Ben Eliezer, that he was not going to dismantle the Etzel, an assertion he made when he knew very well that he would have to take it apart.

You cannot understand the *Altalena* incident unless you understand these games Begin played: yes talking, no, not talking -- all this *Altalena* explosion was a tragic event in which people were killed. This event destroyed my life. Without it, I would never have gotten involved with the Herut party; Ben Gurion sort of pushed me into it. Basically Ben Gurion was right about the *Altalena*, until he started talking about a "holy cannon" [the cannon used by the Israeli Army to shoot at the Irgun's *Altalena*]. If Ben Gurion had stood up and said, with a broken heart, I have to tell you Israelis about the incident of the *Altalena*: the provisional government gave an ultimatum, and with a broken heart I have to tell you about the victims, and let's stand for a moment of silence in their memory -- I would have supported Ben Gurion. But this guy, Ben Gurion, started talking about a "holy cannon." The Israeli Army could have killed close to a thousand people on the ship.

I never told you about the *Altalena*. Saturday afternoon, I don't remember the date [June, 1948], the ship *Altalena* was supposed to arrive in Israel.

On Saturday evening I was sitting at the headquarters of the Etzel, trying to reach the ship, which was somewhere in the Mediterranean. The reason I came to Israel then was because of the ship. All my life would have been different had I not been physically there; I would not have reacted the way I did. At that point in my life I wanted to go back to America and close our office, and basically I had no idea what to do next. I finally contacted the ship, and then the contact was lost. I was very concerned. I entered into another room, where Begin was sitting with Meridor and Landau, and I heard Begin clearly negotiating over the phone with Y. Galili, and I heard that there was a disagreement between them. Begin said that 20 per-cent of the guns' ammunition will go to Jerusalem to the Etzel warehouse, and then it would be given to the Etzel. The conversation ended. I became hysterical and started yelling at Begin, "You are a criminal, you are crazy! What the hell are you doing? This is our only ship, the first and the last, there are no more ships. You, Begin, should be concerned for there to be no discrimination against the Etzel by the Israeli Army. They have more ships, we have nothing. The Etzel is being dismantled." Then, in a more clear voice, I said to him to call back Galili and tell him that you are sorry and you are giving them the entire shipment of arms. Begin looked at me. He consulted with Meridor and Landau and they sort of agreed with me. They said to Begin that there is something in what Hillel says, so Begin tried to call back Galili and eventually started talking to him on the phone apologetically. He said that there was a misunderstanding and he apologized, and the shipment will go to the Army -- we are one army and so forth. I thought to myself I saved the moment, the situation, and then I heard Begin adding something like this: I would like when the weapons are distributed for an officer of the Irgun to make a statement that the weapons are from the Etzel. I smiled to myself, I smiled within myself, and I said to myself this *schmuck* wants a speech, let him have a speech. Galili said that he will inform his people. Then I have no idea what happened -- Ben Gurion and Galili didn't write about it, Begin doesn't write about it: Galili called back and said they [Ben Gurion and his associates] don't agree...Begin said he will take the weapons and ammunition off the boat -- half tea, half coffee. You have to understand that Begin was totally confused.

I spoke about the incident in 1964 with Ben Gurion. He said that he never said "a holy cannon." I asked him why he didn't arrest Begin but arrested me. I couldn't really get an answer from him.

Translated and Transcribed by Eliyho Matz.

CHAPTER EIGHT

THE ZIONIST MOVEMENT (USA) AND THE HOLOCAUST

All too often, Dr. Wise treated the Zionist movement of the United States as a piece of personal property and has bitterly resented any new leadership which threatened his monopoly. His "shtadlanuth" in Washington has been an egregious failure for many years, and not only as far as Zionism is concerned. This weak-knee "shtadlanuth" policy has accomplished next to nothing for our people during these tragic years of slaughter and annihilation.

--Abba Hillel Silver
(JTA: January 2, 1945)

What caused Silver to make these remarks about his associates in the leadership of the Zionist movement was a disagreement between him and Stephen Wise and his followers on the ways and means of achieving future political Zionist goals. Silver was angry over Wise's timid approach to President Franklin D. Roosevelt (FDR), especially the vacillation he displayed with the President over the question of the future of Palestine as a safe haven for Jews. Silver perceived Wise as representing FDR's opinions rather than those of the Zionists. To be fair however, it must be noted that Silver himself did not respond politically or otherwise in a rescue effort on behalf of European Jewry.

How could it have happened that the two most influential Jewish leaders of the Zionist movement in the United States came short of focusing their efforts upon the Nazi massacre? The purpose of this essay is to detail some historical facts and suggest some thoughts on the activities of the Zionist movement and its attitude toward European Jewry under Nazi rule. This analysis begins in May 1942, and traces through to the end of 1944, the period during which most of European Jewry was annihilated by the Nazis, in order to understand the manner in which the Zionist factions and their affiliates responded to the massacre. Background historical knowledge of the movement is not a prerequisite to understanding the Zionist reaction put forward in this chapter, as the surrounding facts will be explained in detail. There of course are many published histories on Zionist issues, including analyses of the Zionist movement during World War II. These can serve as valuable sources of further information; however, nothing I have found published to date touches seriously or deeply on the issues I am presenting here.

As a rule, the American Jewish leadership had behind it very little political experience, and during the wartime it found itself in a conflict of loyalties. Its primary preoccupation at this time was how to maneuver between the Jewish disaster in Europe and the American war interests. A peculiar answer was found: the pursuit of Zionist goals. Among the American Jewish leadership there existed some degree of cooperation, although it was weak in substance. The recognized leadership included people from a variety of economic and geographic backgrounds who sought diverse political goals, to which each remained resolutely loyal. However, despite these differences, the Zionists emerged as the most prominent leadership on the Jewish American scene between the years 1942 to 1944. What is noteworthy is that the Zionist leaders in the United States were greatly influenced by Zionist leaders elsewhere. How could it have happened that outside influences so predominated their activities?

As the War in Europe erupted and Germany entered into battle against the European nations, the Zionist movement found its political goals in great danger. First of all, the people who were being relied upon to rally behind the building of the "Jewish State" were those same people caught in the midst of Nazi hostilities. At the same time that the news about the Germans' cruel treatment of Jews was spreading, the Zionist leaders, on the other hand, with the prototype of the Balfour Declaration (secured during WWI) vivid in their minds, tended to view war as a precondition for political gains. The war continued to drag on and the atrocities against the Jews became increasingly clear, until "by the end of 1942 little doubt remained about the enormity of the Nazi purpose. By this time, the Zionist movement itself was transformed. While hopes and efforts for the rescue of Europe's Jews continued [diminutively], the struggle for a Jewish state became the primary concern of the movement."[1]

In writing about the Palestinian Jewish leadership during the War, Hava Wagman Eshkoli discerned the emergence of two prevailing attitudes in Palestine toward the deteriorating situation in Europe. First, there was the fatalistic approach, which purported that rescue efforts could not succeed because Hitler was not prepared to release Jews. Second, there was the realistic view that saw no possibility for rescue because no political or other tools were on hand to carry this out. Thus, as proponents of either view, the Jewish leadership in Palestine taken as a whole concluded that only a quick victory by the Allies could solve all the problems facing European Jewry. Still, they were in a dilemma over priorities as they grappled with the question of what should be done: to concentrate on the rebuilding of Palestine was their decision.[2]

The chief characteristic of the American Zionist leadership was that they basically accepted both the fatalistic and the realistic assumptions of the Palestinian leadership. To these one more was added, the dreamlike vision, which was identified especially with Abba Hillel Silver. To quote Aaron Berman, "Silver believed that an intensive Zionist effort to win the establishment of a Jewish state was an appropriate response to the plight of European Jewry."[3] One must bear in mind that these three principal convictions led and shaped the Zionist movement in its approach to the European catastrophe during the years of destruction. Otherwise, it would be difficult to grasp how it was possible that a Zionist convention could be held in New York City during the month of May 1942, which did not address itself in any practical way to the European situation. Instead, it funneled its concern into a demand for the post-war establishment of a Jewish commonwealth in Palestine. "All who attempt to evaluate the decision in the Biltmore Conference in a rational criterion will conclude that there could be no worse timing to ratify a political program on the future of Eretz Israel."[4] Precisely at that moment in time, Palestine found itself in danger of conquest by German armies that were coming down from the Caucasian Mountains in the North and advancing across North Africa from the West. Despite this, following his return to Palestine from the United States in late September 1942 (after Biltmore), David Ben Gurion spent the subsequent two years persuading the Palestinian Jews to accept the Biltmore program. In the United States, the Zionist leaders had the majority of American Jews supporting the same political goal within a matter of one year. As Yehuda Bauer concluded, "The Jews themselves [i.e., the Zionists] did not really press very hard for rescue, and their propaganda for Palestine often seemed stronger than their concern for immediate steps to save their brethren."[5]

The following series of topics will help elucidate some of the activities and behaviors of the Zionist Movement in the United States during World War II.

The Joint Emergency Committee on European Jewish Affairs

News of the mass killing became widespread and penetrated the West from the middle of 1942 onward. Jewish as well as American government leaders were among those who received this early knowledge of the reports. But only on November 24, 1942, was Stephen Wise, President of the American Jewish Congress and the World Jewish Congress as well as a prominent Zionist leader, issued confirmation by the State Department concerning the validity of these reports and given its approval to make them public. He did so that same day. There are indications that the State Department, an early recipient of the news, employed various tactics to delay the release of the facts.

Evidence suggests that Wise's public statement on the mass killing of Jews sparked a desire among some leaders of the major American Jewish organizations to work together in addressing this disaster, and set the background for creating a coordinating body called the Joint Emergency Committee on European Jewish Affairs (JECEJA). It included representatives from the American Jewish Committee, American Jewish Congress, B'nai B'rith, Jewish Labor Committee, various Zionist organizations, Synagogue Council of America, Union of Orthodox Rabbis, American Section of Agudat Israel, and others. Although its genesis dates to November 1942, the JECEJA's principal work was not undertaken until March 1943, when it began preparing a memorandum about the Bermuda Conference scheduled for the following month. [The Bermuda Conference convened in April 1943, was called by the British and American Governments purportedly to deal with the problems of European Jewry. Upon closer examination, this gesture was no more than a fiasco of defeat.]

One of the reasons for the renewed activity of this body in March 1943, was revealed in an OSS document released in 1981 in which an unknown informant cites a March 25, 1943 letter signed by Morris Waldman and addressed to members of the American Jewish Committee. In it Waldman explains the reorganization of the JECEJA. The informant makes the following assessment:

Attached is a copy of a circular letter sent out by the American Jewish Committee explaining the formation of a Joint Emergency Committee on European Jewish Affairs. I understand from XXX that this fusion group is being formed for the express purpose of challenging the Committee for a Jewish Army [the Bergson Group]. XXX points out that only the conviction that the Committee for a Jewish Army is dangerously out of hand as well as unrepresentative could lead to the friendly cooperation of these groups....

Apparently the Joint Emergency Committee is not in basic disagreement with the Committee for a Jewish Army on the issue of the salvation of European Jewry. The objection seems to be simply that the Revisionists [sic] are becoming too powerful by virtue of the official American interest (Congressional) evidenced in the Committee for a Jewish Army.

The JECEJA did not have a staff or even a secretary,[6] and it barely functioned as a potential lobby after the Bermuda Conference. Despite this, it did organize many mass meetings nationwide in its desire to arouse public opinion. Its efforts, however, were short-lived, and, in the words of Leon Kubewitzki in late August 1943: "The Joint Emergency Committee for European Affairs I am afraid does not exist any longer."[7] Others perceived the situation in a similar way.[8] Eventually, because the American Jewish Conference (to be discussed below) created a Department for Rescue, Wise disbanded the JECEJA through the use of a political trick. In assessing the achievements of this coordinating body through historical perspective, it can be readily concluded that it did not expend a consistent effort either in rescue planning or in applying political pressure on the United States government.

The American Jewish Conference

"After all, it's your 'baby'. I hope it will not turn out to be a mamzer and that you will have some naches from it."[9]

No other event in American Jewish life during World War II so greatly shaped the identity and political destiny of American Jewry as this single gathering, the American Jewish Conference. It began to be publicly organized in early January 1943, when the Jewish leaders were very aware of the news about the mass killing. However, the idea of uniting American Jewry behind a program supporting both post-War Jewish rights and the political future of Palestine was very exciting and inspiring, and consequently appealed to American Jews. So the American Jewish leaders spent two-thirds of 1943 preparing for this historical event, this display of unity, dealing with issues which bore no reference to the currently ongoing massacre.

The American Jewish Conference gathered in New York City from August 29 through September 2, 1943. It was attended by more than five-hundred Jewish delegates representing the majority of political factions to which American Jews belonged. The Conference turned out the way its Zionist organizers hoped it would. Silver's speech calling for the creation of a Jewish Commonwealth created a dynamic atmosphere; a resolution to this effect was passed easily and excitedly by a majority of the delegates. How could American Jews have so detached themselves from the massacre in Europe and instead focused their efforts and support on such a future-oriented resolution as this, recommending post-War rights for Jews and a Jewish Commonwealth, while thousands of Jews were being exterminated daily? In this context, the question must be asked if, by averting their vision, they sealed the doom for the Jews of Europe. Let us backtrack a bit in order to explain how it happened that American Jewish leaders and American Jewry as a whole overlooked the plight of European Jewry.

The Zionists' Biltmore Conference, held in May 1942, supported the creation of a Jewish Commonwealth. The Zionist leaders worldwide were determined that their political goals would be achieved after the War; accordingly, "Dr. Weizmann then met with Mr. Monsky in Chicago (June, 1942) and proposed to him that he take the initiative in bringing together a democratically elected Jewish representation for the purpose of ascertaining the attitude of American Jewry toward Zionism."[10] Henry Monsky agreed.

In the meantime, news about the Nazi destruction continued to flow in, but it did not deter the Zionist leaders from pushing their goals. They used Monsky, the President of the B'nai B'rith and a crypto-Zionist, to help achieve their objectives. The "…main purpose was to have Monsky, a so-called neutral, to call the Conference and to have it without the American Jewish Committee and the Labor Committee [two groups opposed to the Zionist goals]. It was for that reason that we [the Zionist leadership] fixed the date (January 24) one week before the annual meeting of the American Jewish Committee, January 31 [1943]. It was the mistake of their [American Jewish Committee] life not to have participated, because with them absent, we took over the real leadership."[11]

In the end, the American Jewish Committee and the Jewish Labor Committee did participate in the American Jewish Conference, but after the passage of the Palestine Resolution in September they ended their association as a result of their dissent. Thus, the Zionists won a large victory and a new status in American Jewish life, as the majority of American Jewry now publicly supported the Zionist platform calling for the post-War creation of a Jewish Commonwealth. "Everyone felt that this

[American Jewish Conference] was a great moment in American Jewish life, that never again would anyone dare say that Zionism represents only a minority in American Jewry. It was clear to all who have eyes and ears that Zionism speaks the authentic word of American Jewry."[12]

One thing that threatened the smooth preparations in early 1943 for the Zionist-oriented Conference was the matter of Jewish rescue, which repeatedly resurfaced and disturbed the Zionist Statehood platform. The terrible news about mass killing continued to pour in. It is not clear exactly why this "rescue business" was added to the Conference Agenda in the form of a call for some kind of rescue action; but it was added and appeared to assuage some public faction, although it was not seriously pursued.

The Rescue Committee formed within the Conference consisted of more than 60 participants who represented most of the American Jewish organizations. But they had no idea what rescue involved -- they simply had no experience in this area. Nor did they understand the dimension of the European catastrophe and what had been done or was being done by any other American Jewish leaders to prevent it. In short, the participants had no idea what measures had been taken in the field of rescue since the beginning of the War. Two experts from the World Jewish Congress did lecture those attending the Rescue Committee, explaining to them the nature of any possible rescue and showing them how ineffective any previous effort had been. It was also explained to the participants that they were not to function as a rescue body but rather only to recommend ideas for rescue. Nonetheless, the Rescue Committee members worked assiduously while in session to come up with new ideas. They made a genuine effort to formulate rescue recommendations, to a point where eventually their determination caused their meetings to extend well into the night. When they finally presented their suggestions to the General Committee of the American Jewish Conference, they were met with this cynical response:

> *Mr. Weisman: ...I don't know whether I make it worse or better for the Committee [on Rescue] by saying that they did not do whatever they did in four minutes. They were up until four o'clock several nights.*
>
> *Dr. Wise: Then they stayed up too long.*[13]

It should be mentioned that Wise was one of the co-chairmen of the American Jewish Conference. In the end, the Rescue Committee was ineffective. For, although it was finally organized into a workable body by the end of October 1943, its small impact was short-lived.[14] During this time most of its rescue work was being carried out by the World Jewish Congress. But it did provide Wise with the excuse needed to disband the JECEJA.

In its failure to deal seriously with the question of rescue, the American Jewish Conference gave rise to feelings of astonishment and anger among many Jews. The Jewish public asked questions in its attempt to understand why this

Conference, which represented American Jews, did not undertake to address itself seriously to matters of rescue; but no convincing answers were forthcoming. For this reason, it is unavoidable that we today must ask those same questions. To my knowledge, the best explanation can be found in an article that appeared in a Hebrew Zionist magazine called *Bitzaron* published in New York City and written in Hebrew by its then editor Rav Tzair. I will paraphrase the article:

Many people complain that the American Jewish Conference did not deal seriously with rescue. This is not so. We the Zionists have placed the creation of a Jewish State at the center not because we are not concerned about the Jewish disaster, but precisely because of our concern. We are looking for a worldly solution, a constructive one, to this difficult question, because we believe that the creation of a Jewish State is the only ultimate solution to the troubles of the Jewish people.[15]

This element of a dreamlike yearning for a Jewish State kept pushing forward while realistic solutions for rescue were pushed aside. Again the enigma arises: How could a Jewish State be created without Jews? We will address this issue later in this essay.

Two other comments must be added to the topic of the American Jewish Conference. The first one was made by Conference co-chairman Wise who half-a-year later explained to his friends in the American Jewish Congress his frustration and disappointment with the Conference, which, he said, was not functioning properly and had not developed into an operational body. He called it "a great Tzura."[16] The "tzura", or trouble, according to Wise, was that the triumvirate which headed the American Jewish Conference (namely, the representatives of the ZOA, American Jewish Congress, and B'nai B'rith) was finding it difficult to achieve coordinated action within itself. Wise consequently concluded: "I rather feel as if I were a *carbunum* [sacrifice], with the job now paying an eleemosynary minimum, and saying Kaddish over the American Jewish Conference, which seems to have no life left in it."[17] This was the opinion of the most prominent leader of the Zionist movement regarding the event and organization that captured the eyes, imagination and hopes of American Jews during 1943, and prevented American Jewry, I believe, from responding befittingly to the reality of the Holocaust.

The second comment to be included was made in the form of an anecdote told while the American Jewish Conference was still in session. It was recorded by Meyer Weisgal, a close associate of Chaim Weizmann and one of the Conference architects, who sent it in a letter to Weizmann, then in London, immediately after the close of the Conference. Bear in mind that it was Weizmann, a foreigner and at that time a British citizen, who brought this Conference in America to life. The letter in part reads as follows: "In Eastern Europe ... when a Jew dies, the Chevra Kadish goes to the Bar Menen and says to him, addressing him directly, 'Chaskel Ben Zurich - Zolst vissen az du bist toit [You are dead], you are no longer a member of the community.' Thus with the anti-Zionists who came to the Conference. They were told: 'You are dead; you no longer belong' - that ... seemed to be the main purpose of the Conference."[18]

The American Jewish Conference, a major American Jewish and Zionist project, was planned and carried out only to strengthen the bid for a post-War Jewish State. It almost completely bypassed the crying need for rescue action.

April 1943: The Bermuda Conference: Zionist Attitudes and Attempts to Prevent Zionist Propaganda During the War

The Bermuda Conference, concluded one Zionist leader, "...was intended to do little more than siphon off to some extent the public sentiment which has been aroused in connection with the suffering of European Jewry, and ...no effective action was at any time intended."[19] The Bermuda Conference created an atmosphere of despair, especially among the Zionist leaders, and this despair just strengthened their inculcated belief that only Palestine could be a refuge for Jews. This overriding sense of utter frustration experienced by the Zionist leaders must be viewed seriously, as it was after the Bermuda Conference and under this cloud of despair that their previous ideas for a Commonwealth intensified. It was at this juncture that the Zionist leaders shifted whatever energies had been going for rescue to this effort for Zionism. Nahum Goldmann, a well-known

European Zionist leader who spent most of the War years in the United States as a protégé of Wise, arrived at this same conclusion after the Conference as shown in his statement made in retrospect: "In view of the failure of the Bermuda Conference,... the time had come to emphasize the preeminence of the Zionist program in relation to the refugee question. It was clear that no large-scale asylum elsewhere would be made available."[20]

In the event that the Bermuda Conference had come up with places for asylum for Jews, would Zionist leaders have supported efforts to relocate the refugees, even if it had meant resettling them in places other than Palestine? The answer to this question is not clear. But, in any case, the situation did not work out this way: Jews were not given asylum and the Zionist leaders remained attached to their bond to Palestine. Yet, even in light of the Bermuda Conference's failure to formulate action for Jewish rescue, it is still difficult to comprehend why the Zionists did not persist in pushing for the formulation of some sort of rescue program after Bermuda. The Zionists' politically-based insistence on resolving the post-War status of Palestine arguably diverted their minds from rescue, with the Bermuda Conference probably being a major catalyst in that direction.

To add insult to injury, after the Bermuda Conference in mid-1943, the British and American governments began discussing the drafting of a statement against Zionist propaganda and agitation in the United States and England. The governments felt, unjustly, that this propaganda resulted in tensions among the Arabs in North Africa and the Middle East. When the Zionist leaders learned of this proposed joint document, they worked for at least several months to prevent its issuance. In that context it is necessary to examine why Wise suddenly rushed to see President Roosevelt in July of that year. Many historians have seen this meeting with the President as part of Wise's attempt to obtain the license necessary to transfer rescue money to Europe. It is true that this matter was included in the conversation with FDR. But, according to Wise's testimony, "My real [emphasis added] purpose in going to him apart from the question of rescuing endangered Jews in the Hitler conquered territories, was to ascertain whether there was any substance in the rumor that our State Department or the Foreign Office was to issue a statement enjoining silence with respect to Jewish claims in Palestine."[21] Apparently FDR was not immediately convinced by the Zionists' arguments against the issuance of such a statement, and it took his Administration some time to contain it. According to the Minutes of the Jewish Agency in Jerusalem, Samuel Rosenman, FDR's aide and confidante, became involved in this matter and ultimately stepped in and prevented the issuance of this public statement. Rosenman had initially demanded a political price for his services, entailing the postponement of the opening of the American Jewish Conference scheduled for the end of August, but Wise did not yield to these terms.[22] In any case, the Zionist leadership had meanwhile expended a great deal of time in again not dealing with rescue.

Where Will the Jews Be Found to Create a Jewish Commonwealth?

Surprisingly enough, this question was continually being raised by various individuals within the Zionist leadership; even so, it was never given serious consideration by the leadership as a whole. In a lengthy letter concerning the bleak prospect facing the Jews of Europe sent in September 1942, to Nahum Goldmann in New York, Richard Lichtheim, the Jewish Agency representative in Geneva, worded this question as follows: "How can we ask for that State if we cannot show several million Jews need or, what is more, want it?"[23] This letter, which also contained Lichtheim's pessimistic prediction that six-million Jews would be killed but lacked any suggestion for a possible way to counteract this outcome, was apparently passed among Jewish leaders; his argument against the earlier estimate made by Goldmann of two-million dead was by then already well known. The American Zionist leaders evidently did not take Lichtheim's estimate seriously. While no leaders were known to have challenged it, neither were any steps taken to avert the catastrophe. However, this paradoxical question of where Jews could be found to settle a Jewish State continued to be raised and is recorded in various sets of minutes. In each case the question was overlooked, not dealt with, ostensibly because the Zionist leaders did not believe so many would be killed in the end. This attitude is a bit surprising because these people should have been better informed than anyone else monitoring the situation.

In a meeting in New York City in January, 1943, Weizmann made a political analysis of the Zionist Movement and the steps to be taken in the upcoming year. With regard to the situation in Europe, he remarked: "I wish I had the conviction that there will be these millions to be brought over. Recent events and statements published (by my friend at the right -- Dr. Wise) make us wonder whether there will be all these millions available after the war for transportation."[24] One would expect that Weizmann would have suggested what to do in order to save Jews, but there is no word recorded indicating that he expressed any thoughts in this direction. Weizmann met with FDR in the middle of 1943 and spoke with him for an hour. The memo from this discussion discloses that nothing was said concerning the massacre of European Jewry, but that the question of Palestine was discussed in depth.[25]

At the American Jewish Conference, the question of where Jews would be found to settle the Jewish State came up again, brought up not by the top Zionist leaders, but by a foreigner, Dr. Maurice Perlzweig of the British section of the World Jewish Congress. He had been invited to speak as an expert on rescue. While addressing the Rescue Committee, he remarked, "If you will allow me to say so, the work of this Committee is more important than that of any other Committee; because, unless we do our job, there may be no Jews for whom a post-war scheme of things is necessary. Unless we do our job, the whole question of immigration in relation to Palestine may become irrelevant, so far as Europe is concerned."[26] Apparently, no Zionist leader present had similar thoughts, for, as mentioned above, the American Jewish Conference did not squarely address itself to this question.

The War dragged on, and the massacre continued. When the Zionist leadership came before Secretary of State Cordell Hull to present to him the various resolutions of the American Jewish Conference, Abba Hillel Silver remarked on Hull's negative approach toward immediate rescue. Silver attached the question of rescue to the discussion of the political situation in Palestine, and although the document is unclear, it was probably he who stated "... that unfortunately there might not even be two million Jews to rescue unless aid could be immediately forthcoming."[27] That the State Department was not concerned with rescue is a known reality; in fact, it obstructed rescue attempts. Also, it did not press the British to open Palestine for refugees. When an argument of Wise's was made public in which he insisted that an amendment to include Palestine be affixed to the rescue bill presented by the Bergson Group (to be discussed below), a measure that would only mean the obstruction of the bill, an Agudat Israel spokesman stated his reaction quite clearly in an obscure Rabbinical magazine in which he wrote in Hebrew: "G-d of Abraham, are his [Wise's] eyes blind to the fact that if there are, G-d forbid, no Jews left in Europe, there will be nobody to go up to Palestine."[28] It was only in 1944 that the Zionist leadership gave some political consideration to the problem of "Where will the Jews be found to create a Jewish Commonwealth," for finally they then realized the complexity of the question and faced it more squarely than before. But by this time it was already too late. There are two statements made by Goldmann that relate to the subject. The first was made in New York City after his return from England in early 1944. In speaking on post-war Jewish affairs before a group of Zionist leaders, Goldmann stated that "… the main problem of Zionism after the war may not be the political problem, but rather the problem of manpower for Palestine."[29] But in the year 1944, the Zionist leaders still did not seem to be too deeply absorbed in the question of the plight of European Jewry. Even after the establishment of the War Refugee Board, which certainly could not be credited to any political effort made by them, they continued to push Zionist issues, without facing the reality of the situation. Goldmann's second statement occurred toward the end of 1944 when he appeared before the Jewish Agency leaders in Jerusalem to report on the Zionists' work in the United States. He reiterated to the Palestinian leaders the arguments just put forth by the State Department that the Jewish population of Europe had declined, thus implying, why push the issue of Palestine? But, even at this late date, the Zionist leaders responded by immediately confronting the State Department with a memorandum stating that the situation was not so.[30]

All my attempts to come up with sources that would lead to proof that the Zionist leaders did approach the question of European Jewish extinction were futile. However, a strong and revealing expression was made by a leader of the Jewish

Agency in Palestine, Dr. Bernard Joseph, who visited the United States during the War. When the news of mass killings reached Palestine, he remarked that if too much emphasis was to be placed on the Jewish massacre, and especially if the number of Jews dead was to be in the millions, then how, he asked, would the Yishuv be able to justify its desire for a State?[31] I could find no overt expression of similar outlook in the available records, and this mystifies me, for if Joseph's contention was not shared by other Zionist leaders, then it is impossible for me to explain how the massacre could have failed to motivate them to pursue any strong rescue politics.

The Bergson Group Phenomenon

It is not my intention here to record a full analysis of the Bergson Group's activities during World War II. But a few remarks are necessary in order to complete a study of the Zionist political behavior during the Holocaust.

The Bergson Group was an independent branch of the Irgun Z'vai Leumi (IZL) in the United States, under the leadership of Peter Bergson (given name Hillel Kook), a Palestinian Jew and the senior officer of the IZL in the United States. The group included a few energetic individuals, all of whom were Palestinian citizens, except for one who was Stateless. The group was formed when its members gathered in the United States in 1940 to solicit money for the evacuation of Jews from Europe through illegal immigration, and for the armed struggle against the British in Palestine with the purpose of freeing the country to become an independent State.

While in the United States, the Bergson Group became the most vocal public body which outspokenly stood up to represent the dying European Jews. For their work, the group elicited the aid of influential people both in Congress and in public life. They also reached out to the average American, Jew and non-Jew alike, through their full-page newspaper ads, a major technique they devised to publicize the massacre, as well as to gain money and support from the American public. Their ad campaigns were disliked by the American Jewish establishment due to their forthright phraseology and their inclusion of requests for financial contributions. On many occasions the group was called upon to halt this campaign.[32] The reason for mentioning them here in this context is that they clashed with the Zionist movement in the United States on many occasions, and specifically at the end of 1943, over a very crucial issue, the details of which will be explained below.

The Bergson Group read the battle map in Palestine and in Europe differently from other leaders. In the eyes of the Bergsonites, Palestine was a territory that was being occupied by the British in a manner comparable to the Germans' occupation of Holland and France.[33] As for the European Jews in German hands, the Bergsonites did not temper their concern with extraneous thoughts surrounding principles of resettlement; they just wanted to get Jews out of Nazi-occupied territory, and into this they put all their energy. Peter Bergson expressed the outlook of his group at a House Congressional Hearing in 1943: "Indeed, we are concerned with the

Jews of Europe only up to the point at which they have escaped; at that point they become refugees.... Mr. Chairman [Sol Bloom], I am interested in the people in Warsaw, not in Spain. As I said before, we are completely disinterested in people who are not in enemy-occupied territory, because those people are saved. But we are interested in saving those people whose lives are threatened...Today the Jews are not [refugees]...they were called...potential refugees; they are potential corpses."[34]

It seems to me that during this Congressional Hearing, in which he was intentionally embarrassed by Sol Bloom (D-NY), its Jewish chairman, Bergson explained the major difference characterizing his group's perception of the situation, which was at variance with that of the Zionist and other Jewish leaders, as well as that of the Allied Governments. The Rescue Resolution presented to Congress early in November 1943, by Bergson's supporters in the Senate and House of Representatives, did not specifically mention Palestine as a haven for Jews. This omission was intentional, since each time the plight of the European Jews was brought up in connection to Palestine, no progress could be made in resolving upon any action. This was because of at least two factors: the State Department's and White House's unconditional refusal to push around the British and pressure them to open Palestine for free immigration; and, the State and War Departments' claim that the issue aroused the Arabs and jeopardized the War effort. In disassociating rescue from resettlement in Palestine, the Bergson Group did not relinquish their ideas about the kind of

Palestine they wanted. But they categorically avoided pressing the issue in the context of this Resolution in order to focus entirely on rescue.

However, the Resolution's non-mention of Palestine did prompt members of the Zionist movement in the United States to delegate Wise to appear before this Congressional Hearing as a representative of both the Zionists and the American Jewish Conference, and to express the point of view shared by them. The following record reveals a conversation between Wise and Congressman Eberharter held in connection with this Hearing on the Bergson-sponsored Rescue Resolution:

Mr. Eberharter: And to mix that question [Jewish Commonwealth] *with the question of the present and immediate necessity of rescuing Jews may not be the best thing to do, because whenever you have one simple question, mixing in the Jewish home question ... you* [Wise] *may jeopardize the original intention of this resolution ....*

Rabbi Wise: But I very deeply feel -- and I believe I speak on behalf of the entire conference [American Jewish Conference] *-- that the resolution would not ask for establishment of a Jewish national home. It would simply ask that the doors of Palestine be opened and kept open.*[35]

Despite Eberharter's warning, Wise remained adamant. It is difficult to assess how much damage was done to the Bergson Group-initiated Rescue Resolution as a result of the insistence of Wise and the Zionist lobbyists to affix an amendment on Palestine. In the end, the Resolution got only as far as passage by the Senate Foreign Relations Committee, and it got nowhere in the House of Representatives. Ultimately, however, this Resolution plus other events in the Treasury Department finally led to creation of the War Refugee Board less than two months later.

The conflict and agitation between the Zionist and other major Jewish organizations on one side, and the Bergson Group on the other side, precipitated a bellicose atmosphere and hampered attempts made by the Bergson Group to persuade the United States government to enter earlier into the field of rescue. During the 1940's, the Zionists viewed the work of the Bergson group as follows: "In reality, those who engaged in these [Bergsonite] methods were nothing but hucksters of Jewish despair, criminally exploiting our helplessness and the natural sympathy of well-meaning people for motives we would one day be complex to expose. They [the Bergson Group] sought to destroy the Zionist movement; they sought to destroy organized Jewish responsibility."[36] To my knowledge, nothing today can confirm any of the conclusions expressed above. In order to undermine the appeal of the Bergson Group and its success in rallying the public, attempts were made by the American Jewish Conference leaders to discredit them in a variety of ways. The Bergsonites' success among the Gentile senators and congressmen, as well as other public officials, drove the Zionist leaders to organize a competitive body of outstanding Gentiles.[37] This group was called the National Committee Against Nazi Persecution and Extermination of the Jews. It included the representation of some important Gentile politicians as well as Supreme Court Justice Frank Murphy, who later became its chairman. This group, however, failed to win the mass appeal enjoyed by the Bergson Group; what's more, all the available evidence I found pointed to the conclusion that this committee was scarcely operational.

There was a group known as the Revisionist Zionists that had been in the United States since 1941. The Bergson Group had no connection with them despite charges made by the mainline Zionists that the Revisionists were part of the Bergson Group, which, as mentioned, they were not. Records reveal that the Revisionist Zionist group "...sponsored its own rescue group in October, 1943 -- the American Resettlement Committee for Uprooted European Jewry."[38] I found no trace of any evidence whatsoever explaining what this rescue group did.

The World Jewish Congress and Rescue

The United States section of the World Jewish Congress (WJC) was comprised of a variety of Jewish immigrant organizations; the activities of its leaders reflected their deep concern over the fate of European Jewry. This United States section was affiliated with the American Jewish Congress[39] which was also connected with the other Zionist bodies, and the two groups basically supported a pro-Zionist program. The President of the WJC was Stephen Wise, and his close associate was Nahum Goldmann. The WJC had branches worldwide, two of major importance being in Geneva and Lisbon. According to the December 11, 1942, minutes of the

American Emergency Committee for Zionist Affairs, for some reason or other the WJC in the United States took upon itself the task of responding to the massacre of European Jewry.[40] The fruition of their commitment has yet to be investigated. This group was made up of some very unique and energetic individuals, immigrant aliens and refugees, who were ultimately responsible for most of the work of this branch of the WJC in relation to the catastrophe in Europe. To date, no serious attempt has been made to evaluate their activities and how their efforts fit in with the activities of others in the United States. Nonetheless, a few remarks concerning this organization are necessary to this paper.

From preliminary research, it appears that the WJC in the United States carried on its shoulders most of the Zionists' work in the United States in connection to political aspects of negotiations to aid European Jewry. The amounts of money available to and spent by the WJC for rescue were very limited. According to Nahum Goldmann, "... $36,000. had been raised up until now [July 1943] in the current fiscal period for Europeans, from which $18,000. had been shared with the American Jewish Congress. He [Goldmann] pointed out that since the entire allocation of the American Jewish Congress to the WJC is $24,000 a year, the WJC is thus in effect returning the largest part of the allocation to the American Jewish Congress."[41]

Very small sums of money during World War II meant just one thing: that only very small strides in rescue work could be possible. Later statistics in 1944 demonstrate some substantial increase in the

WJC budget, but the total sums are still very small.[42] In June, 1944, Leon Kubowitzki confessed to some leaders of the American Jewish Congress that the "American Jewish Congress is bound together with the World Jewish Congress almost as one institution when it comes to certain activities such as rescue."[43] Why was there no way to find that money? An investigation should be conducted one day in order to determine how such an event as the Holocaust could be allowed to pass by without winning the benefit of some appropriate sum of money. It is too early to judge exactly what the WJC actually did. But an investigation of this body is extremely important, especially since it carried out most of the rescue work on behalf of the Zionist movement in the United States.

Conclusion

When asked to explain the attitude of the Palestinian Jewish leadership and its reaction to the Holocaust, Israeli historian Yoav Gelber remarked that the Holocaust never emerged as a primary concern in the discussions of those leaders. Gelber added that as far as he sees it, the real problem is that there was a lack of interest in the Holocaust on the part of the Palestinian Jewish leadership, not a lack of ability for them to do something for European Jewry.[44] The same can be said for the American Zionist leadership.

While repeatedly reviewing archival documents of the Zionist organization from the years 1942-45, I found it striking again and again that the issue of the Holocaust was simply not discussed or examined in any thorough manner as one would expect in the records of the minutes, memoranda and letters. There is no demonstrated sense of urgency in the face of this terrible disaster. It is very difficult to comprehend why the Holocaust was not a prime concern of the American Zionist leadership. It cannot be said that rescue was not a priority for them due to their lack of knowledge, or information, or understanding, or because the leaders themselves were not concerned about the Jews in Europe, for this was not the case. Therefore, the answer as to why they did not act vigorously and seriously to the challenge they faced must be explained on some deeper level. The answer, to my understanding, is that the Zionist leaders were too ideologically motivated, and this put them out of touch with the political reality. When they decided that securing the post-war stratus of Palestine was more critical than enacting concrete, immediate steps to assure that there would be Jews to settle in Palestine, they just were not reading the political reality posted in the form of the tremendous massacre. They were out of touch with reality, a fact no more clearly expressed than in a short news item published in the January 8, 1943, edition of *The New Palestine* which appeared under the headline, "Land Reclamation Program Is J.N.F. [Jewish National Fund] Answer to Nazi Massacres." The first sentence sufficiently elaborates: "Delegates attending the biennial conference of the Jewish National Fund at Detroit over the weekend of December 25-27, decided to undertake the reclamation of 2,000,000 dunams of land in Palestine as the answer by American Jewry to the Nazi slaughter of 2,000,000 Jews in Europe."

    Was this effort really supposed to provide an answer to the massacre? The inability to function adequately in a complex, yet real political situation derailed the Zionist leadership from staging protests against the Allied governments, and from urging them to reconsider their negative stand with regard to European Jewry.

CHAPTER NINE

THE HOLOCAUST STATE OF MIND

In recent years, the German massacre of European Jewry during World War II has become an ongoing obsession dominating the minds of Jews and Gentiles alike. For the survivors who went through its horrors, the Holocaust has never ceased to be a traumatic memory. Until recently, though, the majority have kept silent about their experiences. For how could they explain the unexplainable? But lately, vast outbursts of material on Holocaust subjects in forms such as movies, memorials, exhibitions and commissions have constantly been evolving, aimed at expressing sympathy over, remembering and explaining the mass killing.

The April 1943 Warsaw Ghetto uprising has since its occurrence been a significant event in historical perspective, although, but for one Israeli scholar, no one apparently has thought to ask how many people actually fought in Warsaw, what was the result of their revolt, or how many lives were saved by it? (See S.B. Beit Zvi, *Post-Ugandian Zionism in the Crucible of the Holocaust*, Hebrew Edition; Tel Aviv: Bronfman Publishers, 1977.) The symbolism of Warsaw has come to be more important than the actual event – why should this be, except surely in part to serve as a rejoinder to the invalid concept that has emerged portraying the victims as "sheep."

Thus, amidst this background, concepts about the cataclysm have developed and ideas have been formed regarding the roles played by the Germans on the one hand and the Allies on the other, with regard to Jewish lives: while the Germans did the dirty work of killing, the Allies stood back and hardly reacted. The question of "Why?" still remains. So post-Holocaust theorists of Jewish survival now take under consideration the notion that the world wanted the Jews dead, and that consequently European Jews did not have any political allies, an idea which extends into today (see Chapter 10, "Auschwitz, Switzerland and World War II Intelligence"). Some would even go further to claim that the Holocaust can recur, although the basis of their reasoning is unclear. "Never Again" slogans are constantly being flung about by Jewish and Israeli politicians and leaders, bearing witness that the impact of the Holocaust has come to play a central role in Jewish Israeli solidarity, in uniting Jews through their fears and thoughts of past, present and future. This is in the face of a situation where very little fundamental research has been done to explain the phenomenon of the Holocaust in other than emotional terms.

In Israel, the Holocaust is interwoven into daily life. First, it is constantly used as a basis of comparison to the PLO, who advocate the annihilation of all Israelis. Today, in 2012, it is the

Hamas in Gaza. Also, the Yad Vashem memorial for the six million Jews has become a must-see spot for visitors from both outside and inside of Israel, and tourists as well as foreign politicians who travel to Israel are escorted to Yad Vashem. It seems that superficial political gains are sought by exploiting and using the Holocaust as an example of what Jews or Israelis can expect from the world. (Ironically, it must be said that the record shows that the Palestinian Jewish *Yishuv* leadership of the wartime period did very little to rescue European Jews. And if they did take action, they did so along Zionist ideological lines.) The practical political conclusion is that, if such a desecration was allowed to happen, then Israelis possess the right to do anything to prevent a recurrence of their annihilation, never mind actual political considerations. One American rabbi and writer has gone so far as to declare that "the memory of the Holocaust has enabled Israel to be a responsible and restrained conqueror. Memory is the key to morality" [Irving Greenberg, "The Third Great Cycle of Jewish History" in *Perspectives* (September 1981), p.25]. The Holocaust has given Israelis the right to do anything at any price for the sake of survival.

A number of television documentaries have stressed the role of the Holocaust in real politics. In some of these, former Prime Minister Menachem Begin is described as a German concentration camp survivor; and so he is perceived by most people. Begin, however, is not a survivor of German concentration camps. He left his Polish Jewish Revisionist supporters for Soviet Russia and was interned for a while in a Soviet labor camp. Later on he arrived in Palestine as a Polish soldier.

Contrary to the emotional impact of the Holocaust, this topic has never been a major field of serious research in the academic world. This is not to say that many researchers have not carried out some attempts to explain the phenomenon, but most have allowed emotionalism, in many forms, to influence their work and thus have failed to come up with freshly analytical material. For example, there still does not exist even one solid, worthwhile textbook dealing with how the Nazi regime turned from its scheme of hatred and expulsion to one of massacre. And this is to say nothing of some writers who unjustifiably lay the blame upon the Jewish victims in Occupied Europe for not resisting the Germans. Hannah Arendt brought this accusation one step further and blamed the Jewish councils for aiding the destruction process. Were the members of the Judenrat so free as to choose their own destiny? One might raise the question of what Arendt did while in the United States during World War II to help in Jewish rescue.

This leads us into one aspect and probably not the least important which has barely been touched by Jewish writers. This issue concerns the role of the Jewish leadership in the Free World and its reaction to the killing. Historians and writers thus far have hardly raised the question of what impact the reaction of the Jews of the Free World had upon influencing rescue activities by the Allies. Could it be that the course followed by the Free World's Jewish leadership actually perpetuated Government inaction? For if there was not strong and decisive enough a Jewish reaction, then why should the Allied Governments have been expected to do something while the Jewish leaders themselves remained less than persistent in convincing those governments to formulate and pursue rescue measures? Two examples should suffice. The facts of extermination were known to the Jewish leaders from November 1942, and they made little effort to disseminate the information. Moreover, in 1944, while debating the question of bombing Auschwitz, certain important Yishuv leaders expressed doubts over the idea, even in full light of the facts of the Auschwitz machine.

In November 1981, a conference convened in New York City, and there, for the first time, historians attempted to grapple with the question of the wartime Jewish leadership in the Free World. Papers on the British, American, Palestinian and Swiss Jewish leaderships were presented and discussed at length. These papers were eventually printed and released in book form, but few conclusions were drawn. In the course of the Conference, a long debate ensued on the role of the Jewish leadership during the Holocaust. The role of the Zionist movement and its leadership was touched upon, and criticism flared over the movement's wartime concentration on Palestine and post-War issues rather than on immediate rescue. As yet, no conclusions as to the questions raised in the Conference have been reached. An article by Lucy S. Dawidowicz on the role of American Jewish leaders that appeared in April 1982 in the *NY Times Magazine* seems to be a continuation of the

November 1981 debate. The article is basically a polemic, as well as a whitewash of the record of the American Jewish leaders. She portrays the leaders as having been busy one-hundred percent of the time in rushing to save Jewish lives. Such was not the case. Simply by reading Jewish newspapers published during the wartime, one can readily see where and how the Jewish leaders spent their time. A brief perusal will reveal that they were busy with all sorts of issues: communal struggles, Zionist aspirations, visits to foreign countries, tours of the United States, etc. If, as Dawidowicz suggests, the Jewish leaders were preoccupied with attempts to save Jews, why is it that certain Jewish organizations do not allow researchers to study the records of their activities?

While "the impact of the Holocaust has revolutionized Jewish experience as well as thought" [Walter S. Wurzburger, "The State of Orthodoxy" in *Tradition* (Vol. 20, No.1, Spring 1982), p. 3], it is still unclear where this Holocaust revolution will lead us. For it causes Jews to feel impotent, and to believe that in the final analysis we have no allies and can trust and depend only upon ourselves. Consequently, we create our own moral code to ensure our survival, but which instead leads to a vacuum that can only isolate us and ultimately result in our own social, political and psychological destruction.

For an understanding of the Holocaust, if a full explanation will ever be possible, important issues such as the behavior of the Jewish leadership in Palestine, Britain, the United States and

Switzerland will have to be included in the total analysis. We Jews who live in the post-Holocaust era must assess our own values and concepts concerning this event so that we will not fail again to do our part in working to save those who need to be saved; so that we will not exploit it in such a way as to destroy the moral foundation upon which our struggle for survival has been built throughout the centuries.

CHAPTER TEN

AUSCHWITZ, SWITZERLAND AND WORLD WAR II INTELLIGENCE

> *The memory of the Holocaust has enabled Israel to be a responsible and restrained conqueror. Memory is the key to morality.*
> --Rabbi Irving Greenberg
> (I would assume that many American and Israeli Jews would agree with him. "Think before you think...." EM)

Auschwitz: Holocaust Symbol.
Switzerland: Neutral (?).
Intelligence: Marred.

In the almost seventy years that have passed since the end of World War II, among the questions that remain unanswered are a number that revolve around the arrival and dissemination of the information about the German government's systematic operation of mass murder. More specifically, the core question involves the path the information took into Switzerland, and then out to the West -- how it was received, and then disseminated once it reached contacts in Switzerland.

In this short essay, I will present several incidents as interwoven vignettes to introduce some new aspects of Holocaust research in this regard. I leave it to the reader to reach his or her own conclusions.

In his attempt to unravel the identity of the German informants who brought to the West the plan to exterminate the Jews of Europe, historian Walter Laqueur mentions an American by the name of Sam Woods, who resided in Switzerland during WWII and was a key figure in the mysterious and intriguing world of Intelligence. According to Laqueur, Sam Woods was in a key position during WWII in Intelligence circles [Walter Laqueur, *The Terrible Secret* (Boston: Little, Brown & Co, 1980); pp. 96-97]. Although not much is known about Woods, we know for sure that he was the person who received in Berlin a copy of the German military plan to invade the Soviet Union, which was codenamed "Barbarossa" after Frederick the Great.

Many years ago when I started, sort of in total darkness, to examine and figure out certain events that led to the Holocaust, I did not pay much attention to the issue of Intelligence in Switzerland. In the mid-1970's, it was well known to most scholars of the Holocaust that Switzerland had been a hotbed of spying. Moreover, Switzerland was also recognized to be the place where Germans who were unhappy about Hitler's Nazi regime came to unload their evidence and complaints to the Allies -- their hopes of enlisting the Allies' help to overthrow Hitler were not met with too much success. The German dissidents eventually had to go it on their own, and they of course paid the ultimate price for their adventures. The difficulties of German dissidents to connect with Western Intelligence have been documented in the book *A Spy's London* by Roy Berkeley (London: Leo Cooper, 1994; p.93). In it Berkeley writes:

As Philby rose in the ranks of MI6 during WWII, he was increasingly valuable to Moscow Centre as a manipulator of British policy in the interests of the Soviet Union. He was, for example, in a position to counteract the Germans who were opposed to Hitler (particularly those in the Wehrmacht and the Abwehr) in their efforts to remove Hitler and make a separate peace with the Western allies. Such an arrangement would have enabled a new German régime to turn its full attention to conquering the Soviet Union or, later, to keeping Stalin's army out of Central Europe. Naturally, Philby did his best to discredit the peace feelers extended by these anti-Hitler elements. He and his fellow communists scattered throughout HM Government were less interested in winning the war for Britain than in winning a good postwar situation for the USSR.

Dr. Gerhardt Riegner was the World Jewish Congress representative residing in Switzerland during WWII. As a result of his own unsubstantiated claim, he is widely believed to have been the person who met with one of the German dissidents who laid out details about the ongoing massacre of European Jewry. It was eventually Dr. Riegner who did send the informant's testimony to the United States, consequently forcing the US Government to recognize the facts of the Holocaust. Also as a result of this testimony, the American Jewish leadership was prompted to ask for a meeting with FDR. The President subsequently invited the entire American Jewish leadership to the White House, in fact the only time that such a meeting was to take place during the war [see Chapter One of this book]. In the August/September 1980 issue of *Midstream*, I published an article that included comments that Adolf Held, the president of the Jewish Labor Committee, wrote on that meeting; Held's comments represent the only source found to-date describing the event. Unfortunately, FDR, aside from a verbal show of sympathy, hardly took any steps to act to save Jews. Meanwhile, later on in my research I discovered that Dr. Riegner would have been the wrong person to be in a position such as to have met personally with any German informant during WWII, for he apparently lacked the strength of character and insight necessary to take on the responsibilities of this position; in fact, he was in reality not the person who met with any of the German informants. This issue of German informants who brought the information about the massacre of European Jewry is a very complex one, some aspects of which I will illuminate below [see also my "Letter to the Editor" in *Commentary* (Vol. 77, Number 1, January 1984)].

In the course of my research to understand the Holocaust, I ran into an Israeli who, in the early 1970's, was writing a book on the Zionist leadership and its response to the Holocaust. His name was S.B. Beit-Zvi [S.B. Beit-Zvi, *Post-Ugandian Zionism in the Crucible of the Holocaust* (Tel Aviv: Bronfman Publishers, 1977)]. Unable to find a single publisher who wanted to take it on, eventually Beit-Zvi self-published his book. As he and I predicted, the book raised some eyebrows, and some articles about it appeared in Israeli newspapers, but when his book came out in Israel in 1977, it basically hit a brick wall. Eventually, Beit-Zvi convinced Professor Yehuda Bauer of the Hebrew University in Jerusalem to arrange a year-long seminar on the topic of Zionist Leadership during the Holocaust. But Beit-Zvi's assessments were criticized and ridiculed by an Israeli Holocaust research establishment that was too caught up in its own politics. Today a number of historians have accepted Beit-Zvi's assessment of the Zionist leadership. In an unpublished article I wrote in the early 1980's on the American Zionist leadership during the Holocaust, my conclusions were similar [see Chapter Eight of this book]. Ideology -- the ideology of Zionism and of nation building -- was so overwhelming to the Zionist leadership, that no serious attention was given to the Holocaust events. As mentioned above, the problem of how they would build a nation without Jews was an issue that was on their minds, but was not treated seriously. In a very significant revelation in his book, Beit-Zvi for the first time published the June 11, 1944, minutes of the Executive Zionist leadership in Jerusalem in which a discussion ensued among the Jerusalem Zionist leadership concerning the issue of whether Auschwitz should be bombed. Beit-Zvi points out that our very dear and larger-than-life leader, David

Ben Gurion, declared that Auschwitz should not be bombed; he based his reasoning on what he stated to be a lack of information. However, in reality, as many documents show, including the documents of the Jewish Agency in Jerusalem, as well as newspapers published in Palestine, there was enough information about Auschwitz if only one wanted to know. In 1982, I published a book review ["Britain and the Holocaust" in *Midstream* (April 1982)], in which I also entered the text of the minutes of that famous meeting, including the following quote:

> *The Chairman, Mr. Ben-Gurion, summarizes: The opinion of the Executive is that it ought not be proposed to the Allies to bomb places where there are Jews.*

I always felt indebted to Beit-Zvi, who became a personal friend, for his book and for the revelation about Ben-Gurion.

It is well known in many circles, among historians as well as former Intelligence officials and other *mavens*, that the United States was at a great disadvantage in the area of Intelligence during WWII. (For a short summary of this fact, see the "Introduction" to *Intelligence Wars: American Secret History From Hitler to Al-Qaeda*, by Thomas Powers.) The Intelligence agencies were late to be established, thus requiring further time to acquire the right personnel to work with Intelligence and set the wheels in motion. The Americans' approach to creating an Intelligence Agency was first to consult the British Intelligence agencies in order to establish a close relationship and cooperation with them. Consequently, the British opened an office in New

York City at Rockefeller Center adjacent to the office of Bill Donovan, who was the head of America's Intelligence Agency (the OSS). The close relationship between these two agencies produced some level of friendship and mediocre Intelligence, but it also created some major snags, as some of the British Intelligence officers turned out to be double agents for the Soviets, and perhaps even for the Germans [see William Stevenson, *Intrepid's Last Case* (New York: Villard Books, 1983)]. In their broad scale of Intelligence work, the British were responsible for many Intelligence disasters on a number of fronts. Among them was Switzerland, where, especially but not only in this instance of the Holocaust, their failures became evident, specifically in the area of dealing with the German dissidents who wanted to negotiate with the Allies to end the War and eliminate Hitler.

In the mid-1970's, I worked with Dr. David S. Wyman, carrying out research on the American response to the Holocaust [David S. Wyman, *The Abandonment of the Jews: America and the Holocaust 1941-1945* (New York: Pantheon Books, 1984)]. During that time I supported most of his arguments, except that I had a few questions concerning the role that Dr. Gerhardt Riegner played in transmitting the famous cable to the Secretary of State in Washington on the extermination of European Jewry. I wrote an unpublished short article titled, "The Mysterious Riegner" on this question. In the October 7, 1983, issue of the Israeli newspaper *Haaretz*, correspondent Dan Margalit published an interview he had with Riegner on the subject of that mysterious German whom Riegner supposedly personally received the information from concerning the German's program of extermination. In answer to Margalit's question on the matter, Riegner is quoted as saying, "I don't respond, I don't confirm, and I don't deny" any information about the identity of that German informant. It seemed odd to me that Riegner, after so many years of withholding the name of the informant, would still not release his name. This otherwise pointless refusal fueled my belief that Riegner simply did not know the answer to that question because he was not the person who met the informant. I questioned Riegner's sincerity and his character, and my suspicions were confirmed later on when I met with a woman named Cecilia Zimmermann, who had been secretary to Abraham Silbersheim. Silbersheim had founded RELICO, the committee for the aid of the war-stricken Jewish population. Originally he worked within the World Jewish Congress with Riegner, but, due to a dispute over policy between them, Silbersheim was forced to leave. According to Zimmermann, Riegner was not courageous enough to show flexibility in saving Jews through any creative methods, illegal or otherwise.

For me, the second more serious issue with Wyman's book concerned the question of bombing Auschwitz. I strongly supported his arguments on the necessity and feasibility of bombing Auschwitz; the only point of his that I questioned was one issue that had to do with when Auschwitz and its death machine were discovered and made known to the wider world. Contrary to Wyman's argument that the full extent of the information was known only in

June 1944, I think, and I am almost certain based on newspaper articles of the period, that as soon as this machinery of death started to operate at the beginning of 1942, sketchy details of Auschwitz and its happenings were transmitted to the world via various ways and were reflected in news reports coming out at that time. I totally disagree with the absurd arguments set forth in a book against the bombing of Auschwitz that was published in the year 2000 in association with the US Holocaust Museum [Michael J. Neufeld and Michael Berenbaum, eds, *The Bombing of Auschwitz: Should the Allies have Attempted It?* (New York: St. Martin's Press, 2000)]. I often wonder how it can be that Israeli children are brought to this site to complete their education and understanding of the Holocaust. What are they to learn at Auschwitz? From my point of view, this place should be condemned, and not a single person should ever enter within its gates again. A memorial is one thing, but a tourist attraction? How Jews of modern times, after the Holocaust, can be tourists at Auschwitz, is beyond my understanding.

During the late 1970's, I worked in the office of Samuel Merlin and Peter Bergson (Hillel Kook), those two individuals who toiled day and night in 1943 in their mission to save European Jewry. Their work was in some ways successful when in January 1944, President Roosevelt established the War Refugee Board (for further explanation, see my article "Political Action vs. Personal Relations" in *Midstream* [April 1981]). I raised the issue of Auschwitz with them, along with the possibility of my searching the OSS archives to see what type of information the US Intelligence services had on that machinery of murder. Samuel Merlin contacted his friend Paul O'Dwyer, a very distinguished Irish American lawyer and one of the Bergson Group's supporters in the 1940's. With O'Dwyer's help, we received the necessary permit, and I subsequently spent one week at the Carlisle Army Barracks in Pennsylvania examining the papers of OSS Chief Bill Donovan. As it turned out, I found almost no messages from Europe concerning Auschwitz. However, I did find two documents of special interest. One was a "United States Strategic Bombing Survey" dated 25 August 1945, in which the maps in the survey showed the year 1943 where Auschwitz was indicated as a producer of methanol. In addition, I found an OSS document from 23 June 1945 titled the "Memorandum of Information for the Joint U.S. Chiefs of Staff Subject: OSS Operations in Switzerland 1942-1945," in which it was written, "Contacts leading directly into the German Abwehr [German Military Intelligence Service] were developed through a key agent with close connections to high German political circles." To better understand some issues concerning Switzerland, Merlin encouraged me to travel to Israel to visit the former Irgun member Dr. Reuven (Rudolf) Hecht, whose family had lived in Switzerland and was involved in the shipping and supply of grain. What they did during WWII is still a mystery. Dr. Hecht, an avid Zionist and supporter of the Irgun, worked in Switzerland during WWII and was involved in his family business. After WWII he moved to Israel and established the same sort of business in the port city of Haifa. He was an avid supporter of Menachem Begin and his political party. Before I left for Israel, Merlin handed me a letter of introduction to Dr. Hecht, along with another letter which was a copy of an official US document that Sam Woods had handed to Hecht as a thank you note for his service to Allied causes during WWII. It took a while for me to secure an appointment, but finally I arrived by invitation at Dr. Hecht's office. But my welcome was brief: as I had suspected, once I just opened my mouth and mentioned Sam Woods, Hecht politely asked me leave – he had no interest in telling me what had happened between him and Woods. Switzerland, a supposedly neutral country during WWII, was perhaps not so neutral after all.

The relationship between neutrality and Intelligence during WWII remains, I believe, a worthwhile subject for research, for it bears on the whole issue of the massacre of European Jewry -- might the extermination process at least have slowed to some degree, if not been halted, if Intelligence had not been sabotaged, or if some Jews who were free to act, had acted more courageously?

Today's Jewry, which is living and thinking after the events of Auschwitz, should look with objective introspection at the Holocaust event. It is sort of sad, or one might say still too early, to analyze events that just happened to Jews eighty years ago. To me, the attempts to explain the Holocaust by way of Elie Wiesel in the United States or Yad Vashem in Jerusalem, have been total failures.

Wiesel prefers to limit his writings to teaching Chasidic stories rather than dealing with political realities that are associated with the Holocaust. Following his release from Auschwitz, Wiesel ended up in Paris, where he sympathized with the Irgun and knew Peter Bergson (Hillel Kook). Later on Bergson came to Wiesel's aid in NYC after he was injured in an accident. To-date I have not yet seen many references in Wiesel's writings about Hillel Kook, who definitely knew what to do in the Holocaust, and certainly understood the post-Holocaust historical momentum of the establishment of Israel as a modern Republic with a written constitution (which has not yet happened).

On the other hand, Yad Vashem focuses on Jewish heroism in the Holocaust but completely forgot until a year or so ago to include the sole most important Jew of the century, Peter Bergson (Hillel Kook) who, with a few Irgun members persisted in their insistence that the United States Government should take an active role in saving Jews (who but the US would be capable of such a feat?).

Jews living after the Holocaust in the US or in Israel need to find better ideas, deeper thoughts, in order for them to conduct their affairs in such a way so as not to be blinded from the real and evolving world around them.

[Document]

RECORDS OF US CONSULATE, GENEVA, SWITZERLAND

Declassified: NND 730032

BY AIR POUCH
49-Political
Geneva, Switzerland, October 29, 1942
STRICTLY CONFIDENTIAL
Affidavit re Order for Extermination of the Jews.

The Honorable,
    The Secretary of State,
        Washington, D. C.

    I have the honor to invite reference to my strictly confidential despatch No. 44-Political of September 28, 1942, entitled "Jewish Persecutions" and to submit herewith the affidavit of Professor Paul GUGGENHEIM, Professor of International Law at the Graduate Institute of International Studies at Geneva, and a member of the Swiss Bar, in which he sets forth under oath certain information furnished to the affiant by an authoritative Swiss personality of Geneva international circles concerning the order of Hitler demanding the extermination of the Jews.

    The identity of Professor Guggenheim's informant cannot be divulged. The actual material in the affidavit submitted herewith may be given publicity provided the name of Professor Guggenheim is withheld and replaced by a simple reference to "a citizen of Switzerland". I have known Professor Guggenheim for over a year and I view him as an intellectual possessed of integrity, reliability and sincerity. Indicative of the futile search for a solution of the problem involved, and of the character of the "humanitarian" sources one may, in desperation, seek to tap in order to find somewhere the Good Samaritan, I am reporting the close of the conversation which Professor Guggenheim declares he had with his distinguished informant who inquired what eventual steps might be taken to relieve the tragic situation. Professor Guggenheim tells me he replied that he was certain that the Red Cross could do nothing in this matter, but that perhaps the Japanese Government could render service since it is not anti-Semitic and on several occasions has aided European Jewish refugees in Manchuria and at Kobe in facilitating their departure for America.

Professor Guggenheim's informant, it is stated, has taken the former's suggestion into consideration and will take steps to acquaint the Japanese Legation at Bern, and eventually if possible the Japanese Embassy at Berlin, with the information in question. The proceedings contemplated in this paragraph should be kept in strict confidence.

                      Respectfully yours,
                      Paul C. Squire

American Consul

Enclosure:
Professor Guggenheim's affidavit, as stated.

In triplicate to Department.
Copy to American Legation, Bern.

Enclosure No. 1 to Despatch No. 49-Political

Before me, Paul C. SQUIRE, Consul of the United States of America in and for the consular district of Geneva, Switzerland, duly commissioned and qualified, personally came Professor Paul GUGGENHEIM who, being duly sworn deposes and says that

    He is professor of International Law at the Graduate Institute of International Studies at Geneva, a member of the Swiss Bar, and a member of the Executive Committee of the International Student Service, residing at 23 Avenue Beau Sejour, Geneva; that he has had an interview with a very important Swiss personality of Geneva international circles and that this person knowing Professor Guggenheim to be a representative of the World Jewish Congress and to have many relations in the Jewish world was desirous of furnishing, and did furnish, the affiant the information contained in paragraphs 1 – 6 inclusive below:

  1. There exists an order of Hitler demanding the extermination (Ausrottung)

of all Jews in Germany and in the occupied countries up to December 31, 1942.

2. Both Himmler, and Frank (Governor of the General Government of Poland) opposed this order, not for humanitarian reasons, but for reasons of assuring the useful employment of Jews. Hitler, however, reiterated his order in September 1942 because it had not been executed previously. Professor Guggenheim's informant is under the impression that the order is in the course of being executed.

Up to the month of September Professor Guggenheim's informant was enabled to make personal intervention in individual cases at the German Consulate General at Geneva, where he applied to the German official, Mr. Albrecht Van Kessel. Mr. Van Kessel begged Professor Guggenheim's informant to intervene no longer beginning with September since such steps were entirely useless and futile.

3. The existence of Hitler's order mentioned herein has reached Professor Guggenheim's informant through two sources each independent of the other, as follows:

(a) An official of the German Ministry of Foreign Affairs at Berlin;

(b) An official of the German Ministry of War at Berlin.

4. Professor Guggenheim's informant confirms all the bad news given by Dr. Gerhart RIEGNER, Secretary of the World Jewish Congress at Geneva, and Mr. Richard LICHTHEIM of the Jewish Agency for Palestine, at Geneva, concerning the Jewish situation in Latvia except that with respect to the details of the assassination of Jews as well as the number killed, there are numerous divergencies in the various reports. It is only in the essential that these reports are unanimous. Many Latvian Jews are even now still succeeding to escape.

5. The order of Hitler herein mentioned is also confirmed by a Swiss citizen with whom the informant is acquainted and who is at Belgrade, Yugoslavia, and who has always intervened in favor of the Jews. The German authorities told the same Swiss citizen that the Jewish question is one of high electrical tension (Starkstrom) and that it was not necessary for him to occupy himself with it. The Swiss acquaintance of the informant is convinced that there are no more Jews within the confines of Serbia proper.

6. The Jews of Estonia left the country with the Russian Army.

(Signed)   PAUL GUGGENHEIM

Subscribed and sworn to before me this 29th day of October, 1942.

Paul C. Squire
Consul of the United
States of America.

[Document]

I found the following document in the Archives of the World Jewish Congress in New York City, now located in Jerusalem. What follows is the first page of the twenty-page document. In the mid-1970's, while writing my Master's Thesis, I was the first graduate student permitted to explore this collection.

MEMORANDUM SUBMITTED TO THE PRESIDENT OF THE UNITED STATES

At the White House
On Tuesday, December 8, 1942 At Noon
By a Delegation of Representatives of
Jewish Organizations
Comprising

The American Jewish Committee
The American Jewish Congress
B'Nai B'rith
The Jewish Labor Committee
The Synagogue Council of America
The Union of Orthodox Rabbis of the United States

Almost two million Jews of Nazi Europe have been exterminated through mass murder, planned starvation, deportation, slave labor and epidemic in disease-ridden ghettos, penal labor colonies and slave reservations created for their destruction by the German Government and its satellites. The five million Jews who may still be alive inside Nazi-occupied territory are threatened with total extermination under the terms of an official order by Hitler calling for the complete annihilation of the Jews of Europe by December 31, 1942.

Confirmation of the existence of this program of extermination is offered in (a) depositions made to representatives of the United States Government abroad and transmitted through the State Department to American Jewish agencies (b) <u>official German admissions as well as confidential German reports</u> [my emphasis – EM] (c) eye-witness accounts received by Jewish agencies in free countries (d) first-hand reports appearing in the underground press of Poland and other occupied lands and (e) corroborative evidence received by the Governments-in-Exile through their underground channels.

CHAPTER ELEVEN

THINKING WITHOUT THINKING: INTELLIGENCE IN THE AGE OF EXTERMINATION WWII INTELLIGENCE AND THE MASSACRE OF EUROPEAN JEWRY

A LETTER TO E. B.

EM to EB: Your work on Rabbi Wise is interesting. The word "interesting" I know is a bit *schmaltzy*, but I am saying this sincerely. It is a good review of Rabbi Wise's life. In many ways this gentleman had, what the Chinese call, an interesting life. He was progressive, he was a thinking man, he knew or learned how to be in the spheres of the world between Jews and Gentiles, clergy of all sorts, politicians, Labor leaders, African Americans, men, women, etc., and he was loved and trusted by many. I am sure that he had people who hated him, too, but in your work they are not mentioned. Historically, it is very important to know about one's enemies -- as we say in Yiddish, *misnagdim*. And then, after living on Planet Earth for around sixty years, he faced a real, serious crisis. I mean not just a simple crisis, but a real *meshughe* (crazy) crisis, a sort of a crisis that

Jews have never seen or experienced before. Today, the Israelis are almost in a similar situation, but they think that they will be able to handle it; I personally do not think so. Mr. Bergson expressed the Israeli-Jewish crisis in terms of numbers: 1948, 2048 and 4048.

In any case, Rabbi Wise was confronted during WWII with the most difficult crisis of his lifetime. What was he supposed to do? And you argued correctly that he did try to do the best he thought he could to resolve the issues, but because of the conditions that did not favor Jews, his success was limited. You concluded that he paved the way for the creation of the War Refugee Board. I personally do not think that it was he who did so, but your argument is, again, interesting.

When starting work on the topic of America and the Holocaust about forty-six years ago, I asked Dr. Wyman if President Roosevelt actually knew about the massacre of European Jews. And Wyman's answer was, "I never found any document on it." I received my answer to that question a few years later in a document that I uncovered, and even today, as I grow older, I am still trying to figure out the implications of that fact that FDR actually knew about the massacre in the middle of 1942 and later on from a variety of sources, and he preferred or chose to do nothing and take no action. I think Dr. Wyman concluded that this was the worst failing of this President in his three terms in office as President. Rabbi Wise's attempts to convince FDR to save Jews failed. For future historians the task will be to figure out why FDR did not react properly and effectively to this event.

All the stories about anti-Semitism and other concepts of winning the War still do not explain why the most powerful nation in the world did not stand up to stop these atrocities. So what were the Americans fighting for, if not to defeat Hitler and his associates? In any case, while talking about the Germans, it is worthwhile to mention that many Germans came to Switzerland to report the atrocities. I know that you rely on G. Riegner in your work to tell the nonsensical story that he invented that he was the person who met the German informer. The Riegner story is a total lie. I personally confronted him in NYC on the issue. An Israeli journalist in the newspaper *Ha'aretz* did the same. At one point, he finally wrote some sort of an apology.

A few years back, that is, forty years ago, I met a Swiss Jewish woman, whom I interviewed, who gave me some very interesting deep look into this man Riegner. She had worked with him during the War. According to this woman, he was the worst person to be in Switzerland handling this situation, but, as we all know, he did send telegrams to America and to England describing the ongoing massacre of European Jews.

Why is it important for me to tell you this? For the simple reason that the Germans who opposed Hitler were many. They opposed his ideas from Day 1 of his dictatorship. The events surrounding the extermination of Jews made those Germans come to the West and endanger themselves for a good reason. They understood that this type of massacre would put an indelible stain on the Germans for thousands of years. Besides, they wanted Hitler removed and were looking to the Allies to help in this endeavor. The massacre gave these men a good excuse to come to the Allies. So apropos, Mr. Bergson's main argument in the US during the year 1943, while speaking to non-Jews, was, "If you don't do something to help stop the massacre, you are like the Germans." Many were convinced; I don't think Rabbi Wise used this argument.

In any case, I decided many years ago to get a bit more serious about understanding WWII Intelligence. I was permitted to see some of Wild Bill Donovan's papers thirty-seven years ago. It took me many years of meditating on the subject to reach this conclusion: the Allies in WWII, especially the Americans in particular, had no effective functioning Intelligence apparatus. FDR, who nominated Wild Bill Donovan to become the head of American Intelligence, did the right thing, but Donovan did not have the proper skills needed for the job, so he flew to London to receive help and advice. The help Donovan received was both good and bad at the same time. Unknown to him, British Intelligence during WWII was working not for the Allied causes, but rather for the Soviet regime.

This included the "Cambridge Boys" Donald Maclean, who worked in Washington, DC, and Kim Philby, who worked at MI6 in England, compromising all war secrets to a point that when the Germans who opposed Hitler came to tell their story of the atrocities and ask for support to topple Hitler. Philby killed the information.

According to Roy Berkeley in his book, A Spy's London:

> *As Philby rose in the ranks of M16 during WWII...he was, for example, in a position to counteract the Germans who were opposed to Hitler (particularly those in the Wehrmacht and the Abwehr) in their efforts to remove Hitler and make a separate peace with the Western allies....Naturally, Philby did his best to discredit the peace feelers extended by these anti-Hitler elements.*

The Americans had very little experience in issues of Intelligence, so while all the information on the massacre was there, the Intelligence work was a total failure. The Germans sought help, which they could not receive. As Gordon Thomas wrote in his book Secret Wars: One Hundred Years of British Intelligence Inside M15 and M16:

> *In March 1943 a German spy Otto John, working for Admiral Wilhelm Canaris, the head of the Abwehr [Military Intelligence], secretly traveled to Lisbon to meet a small M16 team that included Kim Philby. John revealed that a group of German High Command officers was ready to open peace negotiations with Britain.*

Also, according to Gilles Perrault in his book The Secret of D-Day:

> *Canaris and his assistants did not believe themselves to be traitors. It was because they were convinced that Nazism would be the ruin of Germany that they had*

endeavored to thwart Hitler's plans. They had tried with all their might to prevent a war which seemed to them lost in advance.

Eventually, the Germans who opposed Hitler tried to assassinate him in July 1944, but without success. From my visit and research more than thirty-seven years ago at the archives of Wild Bill Donovan, here is what I found in a document titled "MEMORANDUM OF INFORMATION FOR THE JOINT U.S. CHIEFS OF STAFF, SUBJECT: OSS Operations in Switzerland 1942-1945." To quote from the document:

1. The organization of an American intelligence service based in Switzerland was begun by OSS in November 1942....

3. ...following the attack on Hitler's life. Some ten days before this attack, OSS received information giving general details of the plot and the names of the important participants.

Now, from a broader point of view of the situation, the Soviets needed the Allies to invade Europe in order to take away the pressure from them in the East. The Soviets obviously did not need any deals to be concluded by the English or Americans with the German informers. The British spy apparatus that was totally compromised, did its job very well, and the Allies eventually landed in Normandy without analyzing the Intelligence. So the idea of winning the War, that was a priority of FDR, was a bit confusing. Winning the War should have meant a better Intelligence, but that we the Americans never had. There are many sources on the Germans who opposed Hitler available to you to look up. The second most important issue during WWII was the Allies' strategic decision to call for the Germans' "Unconditional Surrender." Unfortunately, that strategy was an enormous obstacle to any negotiations with those Germans who opposed Hitler.

In any case, the person most important in the creation of the WRB was Josiah E. DuBois, Jr. I once spent an entire day with him in New Jersey. It was not Henry Morgenthau or Rabbi Wise who were important in the creation of the WRB. How DuBois came to do this was very simple. He was of the Christian faith, and Bergson became very friendly with him during 1943 in Washington. They exchanged ideas and information. DuBois confronted Morgenthau, his boss, by stating and providing details of the obstacles implemented by the State Department against saving Jews. DuBois, being a Christian and a man of conviction, told Morgenthau that he would take the entire file and give it to the newspapers if he (Morgenthau) did not go to the President and confront him about the State Department shenanigans. DuBois was still in deep sorrow and sadness when he spoke to me before his death over forty years later. If you have time, you can check out a very interesting book DuBois wrote on the Holocaust.

Could the Jews be saved during the Holocaust? It was a possibility that needed leadership that was not found in FDR or Rabbi Wise. It was a challenge that required steel nerves and a better understanding of the Intelligence during the War. Once we confronted the great historian Isaiah Berlin, a Jew, about the Holocaust. He was in Washington during the War writing reports for British Intelligence on the mood of America. So it was very important for the British to make sure that they had enough support from America. Berlin stated that he did not know much or hear much about the Holocaust during his stay in Washington. Here is what the Oxford University Don wrote in a letter in 1979 in which he summarized his twisted view of history:

As for the Holocaust, I know no more of it than was printed in the American press, and that was astonishingly unprominent; despite Revisionist agitation...
[Pëter Bergson, absolutely not a Revisionist, was the inventor and creator of the Hebrew Committee for National Liberation, establishing in May 1944 a Hebrew Embassy in Washington, DC. In the year 1943, he advertised in US newspapers, placing full-page ads to inform Americans about the massacre of European Jewry. Bergson's work as a leader of the Irgun paved the way for the creation in 1948 of the Israeli Nation. EM]

...the real news of what was going on did not penetrate the general Jewish, still less non-Jewish, public until after the war.

[Total nonsense. EM]

Again, if you look carefully at some of the intelligent Jews who lived during those years, you will see that the Holocaust did not change an iota of their daily lives; rather, they continued living, doing regular things people do.

When I first met Peter Bergson in New York City at the end of 1977, his story sounded crazy to me. So I did some research, which I shared with him. My research gave me some proof that, after all, "Crazy Bergson" wasn't that crazy after all, that he tried all sorts of ways but basically failed to ignite America to act to save Jews. And more so in Israel, Bergson's work laid the groundwork for the Zionists like Ben Gurion and others, to establish an Israeli Nation, which unfortunately is today becoming more like a synagogue nation, a nation with a totally confused Declaration of Independence, no Constitution, and no clear political path to resolve issues concerning its own survival.

As a postscript, a few more words on Intelligence. First, the Military German communications headquarters in Berlin during World War II provided the Swiss with a brand-new type of special receiver. Reports were sent out on a daily basis. Unfortunately, however, these reports fell into the hands of the Red Orchestra.

Second, due to the fact that the British had apparently more experience in Intelligence than the United States at that time, Donovan trusted them with secret information. As a result, an MI6 branch was set up in New York City which became a hub of British Intelligence. But not all the MI6 work in NY City was necessarily done to help the Americans or the Allies – after years of scrutiny and analysis, it ultimately became clear that many of these operatives there were double agents.

CHAPTER TWELVE

POST-ZIONISM

[Document]

To the New York Herald Tribune:

The current fighting in Palestine must not obscure the deep and urgent question regarding the soundness of creating a "Jewish State" as a means of solving the Jewish problem.

We Palestinians react to the United Nations partitioning of our country with mixed feelings. The Hebrew people cannot sanction the alienation of eighty-seven percent of their national territory, out of which two new Arab sovereignties have been carved. But serious as is the loss of territory, the lack of any definition of the human boundaries of the new state is equally grave – even dangerous.

What does a Jewish State mean? Will it be a kind of Jewish Vatican? Will the Jewish government represent the Jews of the world? Will all the Jews in the world eventually move to the Jewish State, or will they become part of a special international nation?

Clearly, it should be understood, we of the Hebrew Liberation Movement oppose the concept of a "world Jewish nation," which strives, through the Jewish Agency, to place the label of "Jewish State" on the thirteen percent of Palestine which has not been surrendered to the Arabs. In view of the fact that more than ten-million Jews live outside of Palestine, and are not in D.P. camps or in danger, but enjoy full citizenship in many lands, the insistence upon a world Jewish Nation is bound to engage many good Americans, Frenchmen, Englishmen, etc., who are Jews, in a difficult and ugly situation.

It is our conviction that the decision of the United Nations offers a choice between a Jewish State as a unique entity, a religious-cultural-political center for World Jewry, or a Hebrew Republic of Palestine, as a normal and modern nation without any ties or ramifications among these citizens of other lands who are of Jewish faith.

The crux of our program lies in a sharp separation between "the Jews," as a religion, and "the Hebrews," as a nation. World anti-Semitism feeds mainly on the fact that "the Jews" are a unique entity. This abnormal existence can now be ended by enabling all the uprooted Jews in Europe, Africa and the Middle East to go to the Hebrew Republic of Palestine, while those who do not go to Palestine will actually become fully integrated in the nations where they now live. The five-and-a-half million American Jews do not want to go to Palestine. They seek complete status as Americans -- of Hebrew ancestry and Jewish faith -- just as all Americans have a national origin and a religion, without any hyphenated political allegiance. According to our program, after a brief transition an entire new structure will arise and the present abnormal position of Jews everywhere will end. In contrast to this, the Jewish Agency seeks to institutionalize the problem.

Their proposed ghetto-like "Jewish State" will only perpetuate the abnormality of the Jewish position.

We are neither anti- nor non-Zionist. We are post-Zionist. We recognize the great merits of that movement in the past -- in a free Palestine monuments and highways will be named in its honor -- but the Zionist program is today archaic.

The Hebrew Committee believes that a public discussion of this problem is vital to the interests not only of the Hebrew nation but also of all American citizens. We feel sure that in such a discussion most Americans will support our views, and that the Hebrew Republic of Palestine will soon take its normal place in the family of nations where it will maintain the friendliest economic and diplomatic relations with the people of the United States.

Peter H. Bergson,
Chairman
Hebrew Committee of National Liberation
Washington, D.C.

December 4, 1947

CHAPTER THIRTEEN

ISRAEL: A JEWISH STATE

By Peter H. Bergson
(Originally published in Liberty Magazine, September, 1951)

The wife of a United States Senator with whom I danced in Washington recently was startled to learn that there are night clubs in Israel. She thought this very strange for a religious state.

A Dallas taxi driver was outspokenly impressed with Israel's fighting spirit, and wanted to know just how we had managed to defeat the combined armies of six Arab states that had invaded Israel. He found military valor somehow incongruous with his conception of "The Jewish State."

This idea that Israel is a religious state is one of the most serious problems that the new state has to contend with, since it stands in the way of the normal functioning of the country's foreign relations. This problem becomes particularly acute and troublesome when the question is one about the relationship between the "Jewish State" of Israel, and, say, the six million citizens of the United States who happen to be "Jewish" by descent and religious adherence.

Israel is not a theocracy. The Republic of Israel is no more a "Jewish" state than the United States is a Protestant state. While it is true that the greater number of Israel's citizens profess the Jewish faith, it has a large number of Christian and Moslem citizens as well, all enjoying full equality under the law.

The emergence of the Republic of Israel has brought to an end the most tragic and evil chapters of human history -- the homelessness and persecution of the Jews. There are, happily, no more "unwanted" Jews in the world, no more boatloads of Jewish refugees roaming the high seas, rejected by all, unable to find a haven anywhere. The Republic of Israel is wide open to any Jew -- or to any human being -- who is fleeing political oppression and religious persecutions.

But many aspects of what has for centuries been known as "the Jewish problem" still remain unsolved. They must be clarified and solved if the state of Israel, and the millions of Jews who are citizens of other countries, are to attain a fully normal existence.

It is not a problem which can be solved by Israel alone. The new state contains fewer than a million and a half of the world's Jewish population. More than ten millions are outside Israel, six million of these in the United States. The bulk of these have not the need, the desire, nor the intention of migrating to Israel.

The solution to the remaining Jewish problem is largely in their hands, and in the hands of the various Zionist and other Jewish organizations to which they, for reasons of sentiment, philanthropy, or sheer inertia, belong. Yet they seem to be moving away from, rather than toward, the proper solution. The American Zionist parties insist on special privileges in Israel and have combined to oppose Prime Minister Ben Gurion's mild and reasonable suggestion that Israel should be allowed to govern itself without undue interference from citizens -- even Jewish citizens -- of other lands.

There must be instituted a complete reorganization of what is called "World Jewry," and of the various institutions which presume to speak for "the Jewish people." It seems to me that the key to this maze lies in the principle of the separation of State and Church which the existence of Israel makes possible.

We should not continue to tolerate a situation in which the "Government of Israel," and the "Army of Israel," exist side by side with "Temple Israel," (a common name for religious congregations and synagogues in many parts of the world); in which the term "Jewish" continues to denote at the same time a religious affiliation, a lineal descent, and a nationality.

Since the inception of the Republic of Israel a new and proper emphasis will be laid on the Hebrew ancestry of American Jews, who should be known as Americans of Hebrew descent and of the Jewish faith, just as there are Americans of Irish ancestry and of the Catholic faith, or Americans of

Dutch ancestry and of the Protestant faith. The relationship of French-Americans to France or of the Dutch-Americans to Holland should be the pattern for the relationship of Hebrew-Americans to Israel.

Faith must remain a matter of each individual's choice, but a national heritage is something that destiny has prefixed for us, and only unhappily tormented or stupid people will try to deny their origins.

I am convinced that an era has already begun in which Hebrew-Americans, irrespective of their religious belief or affiliation, will become even more proud of their national origin, just as most other Americans are proud of theirs.

The new Independence of Israel will affect Hebrew-Americans in the same way as the new freedom of Ireland affected Americans of Irish descent who found perfectly blended their American patriotism and a keen interest and a boisterous pride in the land of their ancestors.

There is no reason any longer for the continued existence of international Jewish organizations such as, for example, the World Jewish Congress. Unless this body intends to become a purely religious one, its continued existence can do nothing but harm.

There is no longer any justification for the continued existence of international Zionist parties, directly affiliated with various political parties in Israel and convening in a World Zionist Congress as they did fifty years before Israel's independence.

There is definite place for the continued existence of the Zionist organizations. Indeed, I believe that the American Zionist movement can undergo a great expansion, but is must be streamlined and changed to become a movement of friends of Israel, open to all Americans who care to join, and not strictly a Jewish organization which is a branch of the World Zionist Organization.

The Jewish Agency for Palestine, which was established under the League of Nations mandate, is an archaic and useless institution. The things it now tries to do are exclusively the prerogative of the Government of Israel.

There is no reason or justification for a fine and noble women's organization like "Hadassah" to be a political Zionist party affiliated with an Israel political party, nor does it make any sense any longer for Hadassah membership to be restricted to Jews. It is difficult to see what religion has to do with an American woman's desire to help fight disease in Israel, or why an American Catholic or Protestant woman should not be allowed to become a member of Hadassah; or why her husband shouldn't be allowed -- even urged -- to join the Zionist Organization and help in developing Israel into the America of the Middle East.

There are many reasons -- political, military, economic -- which justify the interest and help of all Americans in the strengthening of Israel that it seems an unforgiveable sin that inertia and conservatism should actually create a barrier between the great people of the United States and those of my country. Thus, for example, charitable assistance to help the hundreds of thousands of Israel's new immigrants is being mobilized in this country through the United Jewish Appeal;

whereas it seems to me wholly logical that this great agency could function more effectively as a United American Appeal for Israel. Most of the contributions would still come from Americans of Hebrew descent, but as this is a humanitarian and not a religious appeal, there is no reason why it should be restricted to Jews, and why all other Americans should not be asked to contribute.

Israel is now in the fourth year of its Independence, and a modern and dynamic republic is taking shape: a nation which, though small in number, has already become the strongest social, industrial, military and potential stabilizing force existing in the vast area that stretches between Turkey and India.

But Israel's role in the development and the stabilization of the Middle East will be of little significance if Israel is to become a kind of independent Jewish community, instead of a normal and modern nation.

Israel is the only truly democratic and modern nation is this territory. It can and should be, with American help, developed into a little America of the Middle East, bringing civilization and a new way of life to an area in which the Middle Ages still reign.

CHAPTER FOURTEEN

WHO IS AN ISRAELI?

"We have made Italy, now we must make Italians."
--D'Azeglio

Throughout the centuries, Jews have lived dispersed over many lands. They have always considered themselves a Religion but not a Nation, and the world has likewise recognized them as such. This concept originated over a period when Jews lived without sovereignty over a specific, identified territory of their own.

But since then, times and political conditions have drastically changed. In 1948, Palestinian Jews achieved what for many generations had been an impossible and imaginary dream, for in that year, they won both *self-determination* and *sovereignty* over a parcel of the land which in ancient times had been inhabited by their ancestors. With the ruling Palestinian Jewish leadership's declaration proclaiming Israel to be an independent nation, the political status of this branch of the world's Jews consequently changed from that of a non-sovereign people to a new, sovereign political entity. The process was very traumatic; nonetheless, a change was in fact achieved, although in practice its political ramifications still go unrealized many years after the event.

Regrettably, a majority of people outside and inside of Israel seem to view the Nation-State of Israel as an oversized, social community of Jews rather than as a political entity. The cost of this thinking has been the loss of a political identity for the nation's Jewish and non-Jewish citizens alike. Consequently, the most important decision concerning the survival of the Israeli nation is rooted in an unnamed and almost undiscussed subject, which I will name the *Israeli Political Identity* (IPI). This is not to say that the Nation-State of Israel is without many other problems, nor to imply that the IPI issue alone, once resolved, will automatically eliminate all internal and external difficulties for Israel. But it is essential that this matter of IPI be recognized and addressed before a safe and better future with a vision of lasting peace between Israel and its neighbors can be secured.

Israel's current political confusion is an offshoot of the identity problem and can serve as an aid in understanding the IPI. Political issues in Israel fall, for one reason or another, into two arenas: the first is Israel's political relationship with world Jewry; the second is Israel's attitude toward the so-called Israeli Arabs and Palestinian People. In this short essay, I will attempt to examine and suggest solutions to these two concerns.

Israel's Political Relations with World Jewry

Until the creation of the State of Israel, Zionism was a confused political, social and religious movement among a minority of world Jewry. In 1948, when Israel was declared an *independent nation*, a home for those Jews who desired it, Zionism as a political movement achieved its final political goal. In the years since Israel's independence, a myth has evolved which suggests that there exists a uniformity of interests between Israel and world Jewry, a claim which is now especially associated with American Jewry. However, Israelis must come to the realization that American Jews cannot be expected to conduct themselves as though they are living in Tel Aviv, and this concept must be clear to all parties involved. The fact is, I find it dubious to assume that similar interests do exist between Israelis and American Jews. It stands to reason that the political, economic and social differences between the two societies and nations would make divergences inevitable. By the same token, many American Jews seem to think that Israel exists as a protector of American interests in the Middle East; this clearly is likewise a very dubious notion. As of yet, divergent priorities have caused no serious breach in the US-Israeli relationship. But the situation is not static. It is clear that Israeli national interests cannot be expected always to coincide with American or American-Jewish interests, and vice-versa, and the same holds true vis-à-vis Israel's relationship with Jewish communities worldwide. This basic reality must be recognized before a *meaningful* relationship can be built between Israeli Jews and Jews of other nations.

This notion that there exists a common interest among all Jews is a fundamental misconception nurtured by the fact that Israel is a State which is not founded upon modern political precepts. It is the only State in the world that belongs, supposedly, not to a defined population of citizens, but rather to an ill-defined international body of people, at the cost of denying definition to its actual population. The fact is that a large sector of Israeli leadership, both on the Right and on the Left, are prepared to wait, as long as necessary, for the "Jewish People" to come "Home," a concept which is of course politically absurd, and which in practice produces an astonishing measure of political confusion for all Israelis who must ask themselves how they fit into this scenario.

Israel can be defined as a Theocracy which was established by a secular majority. As it is politically organized now, the State does not officially concern itself with, or for that matter, acknowledge, its own people, the "Israelis," as a political or social entity that is significant and worthwhile in itself with its own essence as a nation. To date, Israeli political leaders still do not grasp the fact that in 1948, when Israel was recognized by the United Nations community to be a sovereign nation, an opportunity was given to Palestinian Jews to determine their own *political* identity, or in political terms, to achieve self-determination and sovereignty. It seems as though Israeli politicians do not wish to deal with this fact at all. But this *is* the crux of Israel's existence: i.e., how to deal with its own self-determination, sovereignty and political identity.

Certain errors have been made by Israeli political leaders since the establishment of the Israeli nation. One fundamental failing that has led to this deep confusion concerning identity is the circumstance whereby the Constituent Assembly was abolished on the same day that it was assembled, and no constitution was ever drawn, either on that date or at any later date. Consequently in Israel a body of laws has taken the place of a desired constitution. And although these laws legally serve as a substitute for a constitution, they avoid dealing with many of the Nation's most vital questions. For example, they fail to set forth a clear definition of such national concerns as civil liberties, the relationship between *Nationality* and *Religion*, and just who constitutes its citizenry. Since each of Israel's political parties maintains its own national goals, no consensus has ever been reached on the manner in which the State should treat both its neighbors and its own non-Jewish, yet Israeli inhabitants. Israel's isolation in the region is first of all a problem stemming from its lack of political definition vis-à-vis the question "Who is an Israeli?", which is not to be mistaken for the legitimate theological question "Who is a Jew?" *There was no need to establish a Nation in order to define this latter question.* Hence, if no Israeli national identity exists, then the term "citizenship" is not serious, as it does not include non-Jewish Israelis, and to possess "citizenship" means nothing more than to hold a bureaucratic paper. It would thus follow that if there exists no Israeli Nation, then Israelis are just wasting their time in their desire to pursue self-determination.

However, an Israeli Nation does exist, but it is a Nation that does not acknowledge its own existence.

Why as a Jew and as an Israeli who lives in Israel must one also have to define himself as a Zionist? It is a paradox today that Zionism, a confused, politically and religiously undefined ideology, does not in essence recognize the State of Israel. For according to the Zionists, Israel does not belong to Israelis, but rather to a whole mixed spread of Jewish people. There is an attempt among Zionists to make the uniqueness of Jews, and Jewish life, a norm in Israel. As an example of the Zionist stand, one must only look at the phenomenon whereby Zionist Congresses continued to be held even following the proclamation of Israel's statehood, just as they had been held before this event. One can only wonder whether it would thus follow that if the State of Israel were suddenly to vanish, then too the Zionist Congresses would likewise continue to convene as if nothing had ever happened.

It is not possible, practical or desirable to force Israeli national allegiance upon the Jews of the world. One must become accustomed to the idea that there are well meaning Jews who prefer not to live in Israel; also, that there are Jews living outside of Israel who are politically different from Israelis. This in no sense should imply that Israeli Jews and other Jews cannot develop a meaningful cultural or any other type of positive relationship, if they should so desire. But it does draw a line to the fact that not all Jews belong to the same political entity, and consequently no unfaltering political connection or destiny does or can exist between Jews of Israel and Jews of other nations. Certain steps must be taken immediately in order to effect a drastic change in this state of political confusion in Israel. This then leads us to the second part of this paper.

Israel's Attitude Towards Israeli Arabs & the Palestinian People

The solution to the question concerning Israeli Arabs and Palestinian People constitutes part of the confusion of the IPI. In political terms, the solution is very simple: the government of Israel must give Israeli Arabs a political option to become part of the Israeli Nation. This would include military service or other similar options on their part, and full citizenship in return. If, on the other hand, an Israeli Arab should choose not to become a citizen, then he or she would be able to become a resident, such as the US offers, in which case that person would be required to obey the laws of the land and would be able to work, but would be unable to vote or voice otherwise justifiable complaints of being a second-class citizen. Should this political goal be realized, it would, I believe, effect a giant change and debate among Israelis, as well as a change towards Israel's chances for survival in the region. However, the mentality in Israel today is such that everyone speaks of the Palestinian people in the West Bank and Gaza as a problem, while ignoring the core issue of almost a million Israeli Arabs who carry Israeli identity cards, yet do not see themselves as part of the Israeli nation.

Political recognition must also be given to the Palestinian people. Their political identity has developed throughout the years and has been shaped without question and with Israel's help.

The Palestinian problem has to be faced squarely and realistically. There *is* a Palestinian people! I see no reason to continue claiming that there is no such people. In the long run, the Palestinians and the Israelis will have to develop the best of relations and cooperation because of the geopolitics of the area. This will lead to the promise of a better future for both nations and to the potential prosperity of the region.

The material presented here as a suggestion for a different Israel must be initiated by the Israeli Government. Before this can happen, however, some major political changes will have to occur in the State of Israel. Among them are the following:

- **A separation between Religion and Nationality**. This distinction would, on one side, strengthen respect for religion and religious people and enable religion to be a moral driving force behind Israeli society. On the other side, a constitution separated from religious biases would set the foundation for a workable solution to the question of Israeli nationals, a group to include anyone, Jew or non-Jew, who desires to swear loyalty to Israel.

- **The abolition of the Law of Return**. This act would serve to diminish further *Yerida* (a derogatory term for Israelis who leave Israel), as it would finally amend Israel's discriminatory attitude toward its own citizens. The rescinding of the Law of Return does not mean that Israel would turn its back upon persecuted Jews. But it would mean recognition of the idea that sixty years is a long enough period of time for Jews so desiring to have returned to Israel. All laws of immigration must be reexamined and modernized in their approach. Clearly, however, in any case where Jews are in physical danger, the Nation of Israel would as policy do anything possible to extend aid, bringing outside victims to Israel only if they should so desire. To promote *Aliyah* and condemn *Yerida* would no longer be a matter of the State. Jews of all nations and Israelis would be free to choose where they want to reside.

- **A change in the role of the Zionist movement**, which would hence come to recognize the Nation of Israel as a political and sovereign entity. The Zionist movement might then be replaced by a new body, if such is desired, which might be called, for example, "Friends of Israel." This organization would not be involved in Israeli politics and could perhaps carry out a more constructive role by undertaking various sorts of social work or cultural projects in Israel. It might also serve as a friendly ambassador for the Israeli Nation among Jews and non-Jews living outside of Israel.

CHAPTER FIFTEEN

AM LO LEVADAD ISHKON
A NATION DOES NOT DWELL ALONE

The focus of my writing here is the current Israeli situation, call it the prevailing situation of Israeli mind and action, as well as an examination of the future of Holocaust studies and the birth of the Israeli Nation.

When I was eight years old, in the middle of the night my mother picked up me and my younger brother and took us to the far end our backyard. There we lay quietly in total darkness in a ditch that my father had dug as a shelter among the fruit trees, before he left for the war of 1956. For my parents were worried over a possible repeat of the 1948 air attack on Rishon LeZion by Egyptian airplanes, in which quite a few people had been killed. I cannot forget that night; the fear of that war, of being bombarded in the middle of the night, never left my mind, and consequently the ever-present worry of being again in a war, or endless wars, led me to think differently. My parents survived the Holocaust. They ran away from what was then Eastern Poland/Soviet Russia amidst a German bombardment and the attack on the Soviet Union in 1941. They ended up in the Far East, where they rested for a while in the city of Bukhara in Uzbekistan. As a child, I heard many stories about how my parents had fled in the middle of the night. That event never really left my father's mind, and he took his memories about it with him to his grave. On the night he fled his home, he made the most difficult decision a young person can make: he chose with great pain to escape with my mom and leave his entire family behind. His entire family was soon murdered by the invading Germans. The events that occurred that night influenced him to later leave my mother in Bukhara and join the efforts of the Russian Army in order to take revenge against what the Nazis had done in 1941. When I use the word "revenge," I mean it literally. My dad joined the Soviet military might only because he wanted to avenge the killing of his family. For that he was willing to leave the relative comfort of the Far East and fight courageously, finally reaching the gates of Berlin. He was a sharp-shooter. He also paid dearly for this adventure. He was severely wounded, spent some time in a military hospital, recovered, and thus ended his military service. The Soviet authorities on their part, as a thank you gesture to him, permitted him to travel to the town he had run away from. That was where he saw first-hand what had happened to his entire family. He made his way back to Bukhara, picked up my mom, returned to Poland in 1946, and from there they moved to modern Israel, but not before they had spent some time in jail because of the *Exodus 1947* incident.

I was born in 1948 in Tel Aviv. We lived in the town of Rishon LeZion, just a few miles outside of Tel Aviv, the town that made the modern Hebrew language what it is today (more on that subject later). As a child, I loved to listen to my parents' and our relatives' stories. They were mostly conducted in Yiddish or in Russian --Yiddish I picked up very easily, but Russian only a few words. Of course, the real challenge was to read, write and speak Hebrew. That burden became a mental challenge that brought me ultimately to the Hebrew University in Jerusalem, where I studied Hebrew Literature as well as History. As a young Israeli, I was a bit unconventional in my behavior, because I read a lot in Hebrew. I am not trying to say, by any means, that I understood everything that I read, but I kept on reading. And then, I am not sure whether it was at the end of my military service or before that, I read an interview that was published in *Ma'ariv*, a daily evening newspaper, where the outgoing Israeli Chief of the Mossad, Meir Amit, looked back at his career and revealed the biggest secret of his job. He said that the issue that he tried to figure out was how the Israeli Nation would be able to interact with its neighbors. He categorically stated that if Israel would not be able to pursue integration into the region where it exists, the whole story of Israeli survival would be doomed. If one thinks about it seriously, what he said was and still is alarming. Here was another defining moment in my life that finally laid out a fundamental issue for me. After many years of thinking about the subject, I finally decided to call it *Am Lo Levadad Ishkon*, or in

English "A Nation Does Not Dwell Alone." The slogan *Am **Lo** Levadod Ishkon* is contrary to the theology of Judaism. The more common belief, or the religious dogma, is *Am Levadad Ishkon*, or "A Nation Dwells Alone," which is mentioned in the Bible and has been practiced for a few thousand years by Jews. The Holocaust and the birth of the Israeli Nation stand to contest that doctrine in one way or another. As Jews, we need and must have allies, and these allies must not necessarily be Jewish. I will try to explain the idea of *Am Lo Levadad Ishkon*, as well as to see what it will mean if the old doctrine of *Am Levadad Ishkon* continues.

Like most Israeli young men, I spent a few years in the military, including service in two major wars. To my own surprise, I survived the wars. After my service I tried to resume my studies at the Hebrew University in Jerusalem; it did not work out for me. Close to 45 years ago I came to the United States and received my BA at the University of Massachusetts. At the University I met Dr. David S. Wyman and spent some time with him studying the US response to the Holocaust. I continued by pursuing my master's degree at Yeshiva University. My MA explores the initial response of the American Jewish leadership to the reports of the massacre of European Jews between November 1942 and April 1943. My research was unique in a sense, as nobody before me had looked into the archives of certain Jewish organizations -- for example, the papers of the World Jewish Congress, or the Jewish Labor Committee, or the American Jewish Committee's Executive

Committee papers. Up to that point, barely anyone had visited these archives, which for me proved to be critical sources for writing a well-documented MA thesis. While working to complete my MA, I also enrolled in a PhD program in the History Department at the Graduate Center of CUNY, which in those days was on 42nd Street in Manhattan.

In the meantime, an even more significant event happened in my life, when in 1977 or 1978 Dr. Wyman (while still working on his book that appeared later in 1984) told me that I should try to meet Hillel Kook, a.k.a. Peter Bergson, in connection with the American response to the Holocaust. Dr. Wyman had interviewed Kook at length in Amherst. I do not know, and it is difficult for me to explain logically, why I did not contact Mr. Kook immediately. It took me some time to see him, but our meeting finally took place probably in 1978 after I had completed my MA. At the time of our meeting, I was extremely stressed. My job at the Yeshiva Library was coming to an end. In short, I called Kook's office at the Institute of Mediterranean Affairs in Manhattan, and I went to see him. I brought with me some important papers, mainly copies of documents that I had found in the archives. Many of these documents referred to him mostly with criticism, although not all.

But, I first want to go back a bit. I was almost thirty-years old at that time, had served in two wars, had completed my MA in Jewish History studies, and was ready to pursue a PhD. I had undergone some life-altering experiences. My first real-life event was running in the middle of the night as a child to our backyard shelter. Then as I grew older I began to hear Holocaust stories. I went to school and studied the standard Israeli/Jewish stories of survival throughout the centuries -- the aspects of schizophrenia, victim/hero status of the Jews. Next, I spent some time in the Israeli army with the great thrill of participating in two wars. In addition to all of this, I always kept in the back of my mind the interview I had read with the Chief of the Israeli Mossad, which gave away the biggest secret of his long-life service to the country, that "A Nation Cannot Stand Alone," and we must find a way to integrate ourselves into the region. Finally, while working on my MA, I discovered a key document about the legendary meeting FDR had with the American Jewish leadership on December 8, 1942, at noon in the White House. It was on this day that FDR announced to the Jewish leadership gathered that his sources confirmed the genocide of the Jews in Europe. I was able to publish a short article about this meeting in the September 1980 issue of the magazine *Midstream*.

Going back now, of course, nothing had prepared me for my first meeting with Hillel Kook. After saying hello, introducing myself and telling him what I was working on, he said in an angry voice that he had never met such an ignorant Israeli! He was probably right! After his cooling off, I had the opportunity to open my briefcase and present some of my findings to him. The presentation went well, and I spent the next several years working in his office in Manhattan on issues related to Kook's response to the Holocaust.

Here I must explain something. The years I spent working with Kook at the Office of Mediterranean Affairs led to another stage in my growing-up continuum. Trying to figure out the events of the Holocaust, and trying to figure out the Israeli story, were both complex issues for me. There in New York City I encountered another real-life challenge that especially affected me for many years to come. I walked into this office called The Institute of Mediterranean Affairs to discover another aspect of a Jewish/Israeli attempt at survival. Kook believed that Israel must be a part of a Mediterranean regional society; thus I understood that the name of the organization that he was heading said it all. It confirmed to me the same view that had been expressed by the Israeli Chief of the Mossad years earlier. Over the next four years it became increasingly clear to me that I needed to synthesize my research and thoughts into developing some sort of a political philosophy that would hopefully be able to serve to function if the Israelis and Palestinians would ever figure out a peaceful way to resolve their differences. In the early 1980's, I wrote a short article titled, "Who is an Israeli" to explain part of the problem and part of the solution to the Israeli situation. Twenty years later I published a short Amazon e-book titled *Who is an Israeli?* to further explore and develop this idea. In 2016, I finally wrote down my thoughts on the Holocaust and the Birth of Israel.

So what did I learn from Hillel Kook in the four years that I worked in his office? A critical highpoint for me was to reach the understanding that Zionism as a political movement had ended in 1948. Political Zionism, with great success, emerged as a winner in a political battle, and its objective was achieved – the Israeli Nation does exist. Second is the issue of a constitution: never heeding the advice Hillel Kook vehemently voiced as a member of the first Israeli Knesset, Israelis have never written a constitution. The fact that no Israeli constitution has ever been written created and creates problems in a variety of fields for the Israelis. Simply stated, they have never acquired a political definition of who they are. Being Jewish is a wonderful thing, but the failure to understand that religion is not a nationality creates other issues altogether. The fact that the Israeli Nation does not recognize itself in political terms just begins to explain why the Jewish Israelis call other Israelis "Arabs" or fail to recognize the Palestinians as a nation.

Israel in 2022 is moving slowly to reverse the purpose of its existence, i.e., a modern Israeli Nation; rather, it is moving quickly to become a "Jewish State." I am not sure exactly what type of a "Jewish State" it thinks it should be, and I do not think that the Israelis know what the Israelis want. They definitely, for whatever reason, want to be left alone. It is the unfortunate political reality that *Am Levadad*

Ishkon, a nation dwells alone, signifies the wrong political philosophy. It is rather the opposite philosophy, *Am Lo Levadad Ishkon*, a nation does not dwell alone, that should be pursued. Of course, this political philosophical reality is ignored almost entirely by today's Israelis.

Concerning my work at the office of the Institute of Mediterranean Affairs, I did all sorts of things there, from filing papers to participating in long conversations about the Holocaust and Israel with Hillel Kook. It took me a long time to figure out that while he was alive it would not be the right thing to do a short biography about him. He was still very passionate and a very difficult person to work with. I think that doing the research I did, I was able to put him historically where he should be. He was happy with my research.

Again, I want to return to my concerns as a young man. One major issue I was struggling with most of my life was the Hebrew language itself. The home I grew up in could not contribute to a better understanding of Hebrew. At the various public schools I attended, most of the teachers, except for a very few, were all immigrants who were themselves struggling with the language. Their Hebrew, to say the least, was not perfect. At the Hebrew University I took a year-long course on Israeli Literature from the 1880's to the 1920's with Professor Gershon Shaked. The reading list was long. The National Library had very few copies of these books. However, a bookseller in Tel Aviv, Mr. Lerner, sold me a copy of every book on that list, and I read them all. The books on this list represented the beginning of what one might call Israeli literature. I did well in that course, but, in reality, I did not learn much. In New York City, while working in Hillel Kook's office, I started getting a feeling, or an understanding, of the tragedy I will call the renewal of the Hebrew language. Of course, I am not a linguist, and I do not understand fully the philosophy of language as espoused by Ludwig Wittgenstein, with his acrobatic explanation of language tricks and games.

I once read a great short book written by an Israeli on the development of the Israeli language. The book is called, *Israeli, a Beautiful Language: Hebrew as Myth*, and was written by Ghil'ad Zuckerman. Zuckerman's main argument is that the Hebrew we speak today is actually not really Hebrew, but that the Israeli language is rather a combination of native development mixed with ancient Hebrew as well as recycled Yiddish. Of course, the Arabic language, as well as English, French and German, are also mixed into this soup. To me, the most difficult thing to explain is how, with the emphasis on the developed and renewed ability to speak and write Hebrew, how did that produce a non-intellectual level of conversation or writing which are at the core of Israeli existence? One has only to listen to a conversation that Charlie Rose had with David Grossman to tell how futile and awkward it was for Grossman to try to explain the Israeli senseless labyrinth of Israeli life and ideology.

The renewed use of Hebrew has come with a price tag, i.e., the inability of writers and historians, with very few exceptions, to understand who the Israelis are. I mean this in the political sense, which I will explain. The basic idea of being an Israeli can be an interesting cultural conversation: I eat this, you eat that, we dance Hora, we live in a kibbutz, we celebrate Jewish holidays, Chanukah, etc. -- this all sounds good. But when we come to define the political identity of the Israeli, we hit a fire wall. Israeli has no constitution. Hillel Kook tried to present the idea of the necessity of a constitution for Israel's existence and its future at the first Knesset. Very few agreed with him. Israel today, if one agrees or does not agree, is some sort of a continuation of something called "Jewish." What that "something" is we are not sure. But a modern-day Israel must be a modern nation with an Israeli constitution. The reason is very simple: if we do not have a constitution, we cannot define who is a citizen of the nation. The Israeli political leaders, when they tried to declare the birth of the Israeli Nation in 1948, declared rather, and it is funny, the creation of a government agency: for example, the term *Medinat Yisrael,* which is understood among Israelis to mean the *Israeli Nation*, is in fact an abstract noun which in practice defines instead the name of a government ministry -- Ministry of Justice, Ministry of Education, etc. And there are many other examples of where the Hebrew language is completely miscomprehended. For example, sometimes that issue of "nationality" appears to be more than a bit of a problem in the Israeli government-issued Identity cards: Israeli Nationality has been entered and recorded in such terms as "Unclear," "Converted," "Catalonian," or "Aramaic" – clearly none of which can denote a nationality. This becomes a bit more absurd when one thinks about how David Ben Gurion, an avid Socialist, tried to imitate Thomas Jefferson in declaring independence and ended up instead declaring the establishment of a nation-synagogue. It appears clear to me that this had to do with the follies of language, the consequences of which impact today with the lack of acknowledgement of almost a million Israelis who are not Jews, whom the Jewish Israelis refer to as "Arabs" -- while the Arabic language exists, there is not a single "Arabic" nation. Furthermore, how is it that a political entity, which calls itself "Palestinian," is not recognized by Israelis? It is because the Israelis do not recognize themselves as Israelis.

These are complex issues that need to be resolved: Who are the Israelis? Are they a new nation that political Zionism created and successfully resolved, or are they a nation that does not know that it is actually a nation because it cannot define itself? As long as Israel has no constitution, one cannot be certain whom the Israelis represent and who they are. And more, the study I took upon myself to figure out, i.e., what was the actual response of the American Jewish leadership to the Holocaust, taught me that the American Jewish leadership suffered from an old disease, called ideology: thinking about the future and forgetting the present provided them, for whatever reason, a path they chose that had nothing to do with the European Jewish crisis. The Zionist ideology provided a path for the Jewish leadership to do almost nothing to save European Jews. It is the same today -- we Jews have no clue politically where we are going. We are caught in political/ideological limbo. Israel cannot be a "Jewish State," the same as the USA cannot be the United States of Christian America.

I could tell more about what I learned from Hillel Kook, but I will leave that to another occasion.

EPILOGUE

THERE IS NO MONUMENT TO THE NATIVE AMERICAN INDIAN

*A Tribute To Will Rogers, Jr.,
A Forgotten Holocaust Hero*

On the New York City urban shore
    there is no monument to the Native American Indian

On the sandy golden shores of Tel Aviv
    there is no monument to the Native American Indian

On the rocky grey granite shore of Boston
    there is no monument to the Native American Indian

On the sandy yellow beaches of Los Angeles
    there is no monument to the Native American Indian

At the Washington Holocaust Memorial
    there is no monument to the Native American Indian

At the Yad Vashem Holocaust Memorial in Jerusalem
    there is no monument to the Native American Indian

There is no monument to Will Rogers, Jr.
    the Native American Indian
    in the Arizona desert where he died by suicide

There are not enough monuments on Planet Earth
    for the WWII victims

There are not enough marble tomb stones
    to remember the Jews who died in the Holocaust

There are not enough memorial days
    to commemorate all those victims

Now that "Auschwitz"
    is almost a common word
Now, so many years after Auschwitz
    we supposedly should understand what Auschwitz meant --
    we don't
For those who deny that Auschwitz existed
For those who remember that Auschwitz existed
To all those institutions of memory
To all those beautiful cities which lie near big seas
    from the Atlantic shores
    to the Pacific shores
    to the Mediterranean shores

Let's not forget this

Jews were the main victims of the Holocaust

So we ask -- did anybody care?
So we ask -- does anybody remember?
So we ask -- what happened to us as human beings?

Wasn't there a soul, a person
an individual who really cared?
an individual who tried to stop it?

After so many years
        after so many books, after so many movies,
after so many writers
        after so many television shows, after so many discussions
--we seem to forget, we seem to forget
        the Native American Indian Will Rogers, Jr.
                the son of the famous humorist, actor,
                descendant and ancestor of Cherokee Indians
        Will Rogers, Sr., who always reminded people
                that his forefathers were not on the Mayflower,
                but rather were the people there to welcome the Mayflower
Will Rogers, Sr., whose immortal political analysis of American politics
must not be forgotten:
every Congress begins with a Prayer,

              and ends with an Investigation

Will Rogers, Sr., the father of Will Rogers, Jr.
       brought into this world an individual, a
       person, who
in the midst of the Holocaust
in the depth of darkness
in the year 1943
on the Potomac
while a Congressman from California
tried to convince America
stood up to convince America
that its role in the War
as the most powerful nation on Planet Earth
should be to save Jews

On Capitol Hill
       Will Rogers, Jr., raised his voice and
suggested
              with a political proposal,
              that Roosevelt
              the American President
                      should focus on saving Jews
And in the middle of 1943
       he traveled to England to convince the
British Government
              that they should save Jews
He came back disappointed

At the end of 1943
       he presented a resolution in Congress
             again to save Jews
              again to get America involved

But he failed

At the end of 1943
       he went to Europe
              to fight against the Nazis
                     and returned a decorated hero

Will Rogers, Jr., was a Native American Indian

This is the story of the Native American Indian
       whom we all seem to forget
This is the story of the Native American Indian
       who has no monument
This is the story of the Native American Indian
       whom we Jews and Gentiles should never forget

This is the monument that Jews and Gentiles should build
       in all those aforementioned cities

   So we will never forget this Native American Indian

                Eliyo Matz, International Holocaust Day,
                            January 27, 2020.

APPENDICES

APPENDIX A

LETTER FROM DR. STEPHEN S. WISE

(Copy)
December 27 (?), 1943
(Letterhead of American Jewish Conference,
330 West 42nd Street, N.Y.C.)
From the Office of Dr. Stephen S. Wise
40 West 68th Street

Hon. Harold Ickes
Department of the Interior
Washington, D.C.

Dear Friend Ickes:

      I was very sorry to note, as were others among your friends, that you had accepted the chairmanship of the Washington Division of the Committee to Rescue European Jews. I am enclosing a copy of a statement about to be issued by the American Jewish Conference which virtually includes all organized, responsible and representative Jewish groups and organizations in America.

      I do not like to speak ill to you, not of us, concerning a group of Jews, but I am under the inexorable necessity of saying to you that the time will come and come soon when you will find it necessary to withdraw from this irresponsible group which exists and obtains funds through being permitted to use the names of non-Jews like yourself.

I wish I could have seen you before you gave your consent. I know that your aim is to save Jews, but why tie up with an organization which talks about saving Jews, gets a great deal of money for saving them, but, in my judgement, has not done a thing which may result in the saving of a single Jew.

Faithfully yours,

(sgd) S.S. Wise

President

APPENDIX B

PRESS RELEASE FROM DR. STEPHEN S. WISE

[This press release appeared on the front page of the Intermountain Jewish News of Denver on December 10, 1943.]

WISE CALLS RESCUE BILL 'INADEQUATE'

Dr. Stephen S. Wise, co-chairman of the American Jewish Conference, appearing as a witness at the hearings of the House Foreign Affairs Committee, described as "inadequate" the Rogers-Baldwin resolution recommending that the president establish a committee of experts to formulate plans for the rescue of European Jewry. The resolution is sponsored by the Emergency Committee to Save the Jewish People of Europe....

APPENDIX C

NEWS REPORT FROM PM MAGAZINE – NOVEMBER 25, 1942

NEWS FROM ABROAD

Hitler Orders Murder of All Europe's Jews

PM's Bureau

WASHINGTON, Nov. 25 – Rabbi Stephen S.Wise of New York stated flatly after a conference with State Dept. officials yesterday that Hitler has ordered extermination of all Jews in German-occupied Europe by the end of this year.

He said reports to this effect had been reaching Jewish agencies in this country for some time, but that confirmation had been lacking until now. He said he had received from the State Dept. documentary evidence supporting the reports.

He quoted an unidentified European emissary of the President, speaking of the reported programs, thus:

"Your worst fears are true."

Dr. Wise said information in his possession, presumably affidavits collected at his request by the State Dept.'s European representatives, led him to believe that 2,500,000 of the 5,000,000 Jews in Occupied Europe already had been exterminated.

"This is one of the last mad acts of destruction this man will perpetrate before he is called to judgement," the Rabbi said.

HITLER IN RAGE

He said he also had information indicated that Hitler was in a rage against subordinates because the process of Jewish extermination was not proceeding fast enough to suit him.

Dr. Wise said Warsaw, the capital of Poland, afforded a fair example of what has been done to the Jews. There the Jewish population was reduced from 500,000 to 140,000 and rations for remaining Jews were issued on the assumption that only 100,000 survived.

He said that when Nazi leaders speak of exterminating Jews in Poland, they speak of four-fifths of the Jewish population in Occupied Europe, because many are either now in Poland or are being shipped there under a regrouping plan.

Various methods of murder have been employed, Dr. Wise said, including poison, asphyxiation and injection of an air bubble into the victim's blood stream. This last method, he said, has become common. He said, "One Nazi physician can handle more than 100 men an hour by this method."

APPENDIX D

NEWS REPORT FROM UNITED PRESS

12 – THE WASHINGTON DAILY NEWS, FRIDAY, MAY 19, 1944

Hebrew 'Embassy' Here
Castigated by Zionists

By United Press

The Zionist organizations today denounced as a "fraud," "buffoonery," and "comic opera drollery if it were not so tragic" the bid of the Hebrew Committee of National Liberation for recognition as temporary trustee of "the Hebrew nation's interests."

The criticism by the established Jewish organizations had been predicted earlier when Peter H. Bergson, head of the new committee, formally announced its formation at its new headquarters – a $63,000 mansion at 2315 Massachusetts-av nw.

Bergson proclaimed the "rebirth of the Hebrew nation" after 1809 years of Hebrew dispersion over the world and announced this his committee would seek:

SEEK $1,000,000
1. Recognition as one of the United Nations.

2. Representation on the Inter-Allied Commission on War Crimes.

3. A seat on the United Nations relief and rehabilitation administration board.

4. The right for tens of thousands of Hebrews to fight the Nazis in their own name – as the Hebrew Army.

Bergson also announced that the committee would attempt at once to sell $1,000,000 worth of free Palestine bonds to the American public. He said the committee had been financed so far by interested persons who also had advanced the $63,000 purchase for the former Iranian Embassy building.

In the diplomatic field, in addition to seeking recognition similar to that granted to the French Committee of National Liberation, the Hebrew Committee will soon issue a formal diplomatic note to the U.S. stating its aims.

Bergson and seven other members of the committee emphasized that they did not claim to speak for U.S. Hebrews, but only for those in Palestine and occupied Europe.

Even so, the American Zionist organizations immediately ridiculed the committee's proposals. Dr. Israel Goldstein, Zionist Organization of America president, said that the committee was composed of "a self-appointed group of four or five irresponsible young men" who have equipped themselves with a toga of "trusteeship of the Hebrew Nation."

NO NEW 'MOSES'

"The extent to which the previous undertakings by this small group of boys has already succeeded in misleading a gullible public must have gone to their heads," he said.

Dr. Leon Feuer, Washington Bureau of the American Zionist Emergency Council director, said: "Every movement has its lunatic fringe and irresponsible splinter factions. The danger is that an uninformed people may be taken in and may be led to believe that a new Moses has arisen in Israel."

Dr. Nahum Goldmann, representative of the Jewish Agency for Palestine, charged that the committee was a "fraud."

APPENDIX E

AN ADDRESS

By Peter H. Bergson, Chairman
Hebrew Committee of National Liberation

Delivered at the Town Hall, New York City
and Broadcast over Radio Station W Q X R
July 19, 1944
Under the Auspices of the
American League for a Free Palestine

You are all aware of the gruesomeness of the disaster that has befallen our people. You also know that it has not come suddenly, but that it is the culmination of long decades of persecution and pogroms; yet nothing really complete and drastic has been suggested as a remedy. All that the Jews the world over had to counteract Germany's savage might was confusion and wishful thinking.

And even today, after three years of wholesale massacre, when out of some eight million Jews in Europe only five millions survive, that confusion still prevails, that same *status quo* of centuries, which has made the Jews a chosen people – chosen for discrimination and abuse.

We abhor the fact that nothing new was done. Worse than that, nothing new had even been proposed, despite our three million dead. We believe that the present structure of the organization of the Jews the world over, which has led to the present catastrophe, must give way to a new system under which there may be hope for survival.

Let me say that it was the Jews who have clung to the *status quo*. Let me say further that it was the so-called leaders who have lulled us from disaster to disaster by glib oratory about the unity of the Jewish people, and who kept pointing out to us that we survived all tyrannies before.

I condemn these easygoing preachers. I condemn them, for they were never there. They preached *status quo* not from the ruins of Warsaw, the ghettoes of Bucharest or Budapest, but from the security of New York or Philadelphia or Cleveland.

Yes, there has always been a Jewish people and there always will be one, but this is abstract rhetoric which did not save the millions of our dead and will not save those remaining.

Of course, I agree that spiritually, and academically, we are all Jews. But practically speaking, American Jews are members of a great, mighty and free nation, the United States of America; the Jews of Warsaw or Bucharest, like myself, for example, are members of another nation. For the Hebrew people of Europe and Palestine have been remolded into one entity and are in fact one nation – the Hebrew nation. It is because this nation has not yet been formally recognized that the disaster which has befallen it has been so vast, and the way for remedy blocked.

We must not permit the confusion resulting from 1800 years of abnormal existence to continue to stand in the way. Some of the dispersed Hebrews accepted other nationality and assumed allegiance to other nations, thus becoming an integral part of those nations. Others clung steadfastly to their Hebrew nationality: they have always regarded themselves – and have been regarded by others – as Hebrews in exile.

It is these Hebrew people, living mostly in Europe and Palestine, who factually constitute the Hebrew Nation. Consequently Hebrew nationality does not embrace Englishmen who practice the Jewish religion, it most certainly does not embrace the millions of Americans, commonly referred to as Jews, who are actually Americans of Hebrew descent and of the Jewish religion. They do not belong to the Hebrew Nation any more than President Roosevelt belongs to the Dutch nation or Mr. Willkie belongs to the German nation. These "American Jews" are Americans first, last, and always. Their ancestors, way back 2,000 years ago, were Hebrews. Justice Frankfurter is not a Hebrew. He is an American of Jewish descent, practicing the Jewish religion, exactly as Justice Murphy is an American of Irish descent, practicing the Catholic religion. Mr. Frankfurter can perhaps acquire Hebrew citizenship by renouncing his allegiance to the United States, if he wishes. But no matter how hard he wished, he could not have both American *and* Hebrew nationality.

This might be an abstract and academic problem so far as Justice Frankfurter and the other millions of Americans of Hebrew descent are concerned. To the Hebrew Nation in Europe this is a problem of the gravest urgency and reality. Indeed, it is a problem of life and death. The Hungarian Jews are crying out for the salvation implicit in this solution. They demand recognition as citizens of the Hebrew Nation. Only this will take them out of the jurisdiction of the Axis and place them under the protection of the Red Cross and a neutral Protective Power.

The Hebrew Nation has had 3,000,000 casualties. This is 35 per cent of its population. Proportionately, this would mean 20,000,000 British casualties; 45,000,000 American casualties. In the face of such a disaster, we have no right to be timid and frightened by new realities or new formulas. Added to our long history, these 3,000,000 casualties out of 8,000,000 have remolded the surviving 5,000,000 into the renascent Hebrew Nation.

It is as a nation that we are being attacked and massacred and it is therefore only as a nation that we can be saved. It is an evil formula which insists on calling us German, Rumanian, or Hungarian Jews, and regarding us as individuals under the laws of these nations. It is worse to persist in calling us Stateless Jews and placing us outside the law of any nation. It is this *status quo* more than any other single thing which is responsible for our horrible position today.

The first thing that must be done is to recognize us as a nation amongst the nations of the world, for without this recognition we can have no representative to speak for us on a level of parity with representatives of other nations. We cannot get representation on commissions or conferences of nations. Thus the one flag conspicuously and tragically missing amongst the 42 United Nations' banners is the Hebrew. Thus our flag does not wave over the Palestine Regiment when it marches into battle, and the graves of Hebrew heroes who die fighting Nazis are not marked with the insignia for which they lived and died, but are marked with the insignia of foreign nations.

Furthermore, thousands upon thousands of Hebrews now referred to as "Stateless Jews" are still immobilized and have no opportunity at all to fight our Nazi enemy.

It is because the Hebrew Nation is not recognized that its representatives were absent when 42 nations gathered in Atlantic City to map plans for United Nations relief and rehabilitation. It is this lack of recognition which is responsible for the paradoxical situation of our not being represented on the Inter-Allied Commission on War Crimes in London, although it was against us that 80 per cent of those crimes were committed.

It is because of this that our problem has never received any international consideration which was in any way commensurate with the magnitude of the problem.

We can no longer tolerate the situation which distinguishes the Hebrew people of Europe merely as 5,000,000 human beings marked for slaughter by the barbarous Nazis. We much insist on their recognition as a positive entity: as a full partner in the world struggle for descent [sic] humanity. Our dead must no longer be considered merely as useless victims of Nazi bestiality. They must be recognized for what they are – honored casualties of the United Nations' common war for freedom.

Our soldiers have fought and killed Germans and died in some of the epic battles of this war. The 28-day battle of the Warsaw ghetto ranks with Dunkirk, Stalingrad, and Tarawa. (This is not my appraisal but that of an editorial in the New York *Times*.) The ghetto of Bialystok was another heroic battlefront. Some of Europe's fiercest, most indomitable fighters today are Hebrew guerrilla bands, daily harassing German battle lines and communications. Should they be denied recognition merely because they are outnumbered by the Nazis a thousand to one? And then there are the fighting Hebrews of Palestine – 30,000 of whom fought and died in Greece, in Egypt, in Libya, in Tunisia, in Abyssinia, and are today fighting with your gallant Fifth Army in Italy.

The Hebrew Nation's casualties alone exceed the total populations of some of the United Nations. Yet these small nations are treated as honorable and equal partners. We are treated as miserable and pitiful victims.

If you view the situation as factually and as dispassionately as possible, you will find that while the Germans are murdering Hebrew people at the rate of *thousands per day*, the War Refugee Board, the Intergovernmental Committee on Refugees and the many private charitable organizations combined are rescuing at most several *hundreds* per *month*.

But despite this horrible disproportion, the old organizations, operating under the same old formulas, but dominated by weakness and inertia, are holding on to the *status quo*. Their intentions may be of the best, but for them this *status quo* means life and liberty in a free country. For the Hebrew people in Europe the *status quo* means death and humiliation.

In this intolerable situation, it is only natural that some Hebrews who managed to escape from Warsaw took the initiative to formulate a plan. It has one tremendous overriding value -- it is new, it is different, and it shatters the *status quo*. Hence it offers a hope of life and dignity.

The proposals of the Hebrew Committee of National Liberation have drawn sharp and bitter abuse. But is there an alternative proposal? None has been advanced. All there is, is the same old hush-hush, do-nothing policy based on wishful thinking and unctuous preaching. The tragedy of this is that the preaching is done in the comfort and security of America, at the expense of the Hebrews in the depths of misery and despair in Europe.

I present a summary of what the Hebrew Committee of National Liberation proposes, in the cold, diplomatic language in which it was offered to Secretary of State Cordell Hull in an official communication:

  (a) Recognition of the Hebrew Nation as a co-belligerent ally in the war against the Axis and as a member of the United Nations.

  (b) Participation and representation of the Hebrew Nation on the Inter-Allied Commission on War Crimes, the United Nations Relief and Rehabilitation Administration, and all other councils of the United Nations in which the interests of the Hebrew people are involved.

(c) Acknowledgement of the participation of the Hebrew Nation on the field of battle through the unification of the Hebrew-Palestinian units of the British Army, of the many fighting Hebrews now enrolled a "stateless" in the forces of various United Nations, and of the Hebrew underground forces into a Hebrew Army to fight under Allied command and with a status similar to that of the other United Nations overrun by Germany.

(d) Admission into emergency rescue shelters of every Hebrew escaping from Nazi mass murder who reaches the shores of Palestine.

We further propose that the United Nations recognize the Hebrew Committee of National Liberation as the temporary representative of our Nation. Once such recognition is within view, the present composition of the Committee, which I am privileged and honored to head, would be expanded to include additional representative Hebrews from both Palestine and Europe.

Our proposals are directed toward the United Nations. They can very easily act upon them if they so desire. If they do not, it is for the reason that they do not wish to do so.

I must say in all fairness to the governments of the United Nations, that not they alone are to be blamed for the present horrible condition of our people. As men and as decent men, we must first of all blame ourselves. I reiterate: It is the abnormality of our position which is responsible, and it is we who are responsible for allowing this abnormality to continue. Until the formation of the Hebrew Committee of National Liberation, not a semblance of a practical political program existed, not one attempt at realistic political international negotiation was made.

It was not the right to worship God in their own way that we needed to secure for our people in Europe. It was not religious excommunication that we needed to have others impose on the Nazis as punishment. It was a political status and the right to live, it was the diplomatic and military might of the United Nations that had to be mobilized.

Yet how and through whom have we attempted to secure such governmental action? Through a maze of religious or charitable organizations without political statue whatsoever. Secretary of State Hull, with the best of intentions in the world – which from conversations with him I know he has – cannot possibly negotiate with Rabbi Wise, for example, or with any other American citizen, on international political matters, in which that American citizen purports to represent another nation. Consequently, the scores of Jewish delegations received by Secretary Hull are regarded by him as visiting compatriots; he listens to them as to constituents pleading for distant friends in distress. Such visits could not therefore produce serious results in the field of international diplomacy and warfare. This is true in the case of Dr. Weizmann – an Englishman – in his conversations with *his* government.

The United States and Great Britain have officially confirmed reports that the Germans have killed with poison gas 1,000,000 Hebrews of Europe. Who is there to demand that Mr. Roosevelt and Mr. Churchill make good of their oft-repeated warning of retaliation in kind for the use of poison gas against any member of the United Nations? Yet, one million poison gas casualties, more than double the total of American and British war casualties, have evoked nothing, because it is not the business of American clergymen – and Dr. Wise is just an American clergyman – to tell their government to use poison gas. We of the Hebrew Committee of National Liberation, whose province it is to do so, demand that the American and British governments first warn, and then act, in kind, against this depraved practice.

Another example is the negotiations between Dr. Weizmann, President of the World Zionist Organization, and the British Government as the Mandatory Power for

Palestine. Dr. Weizmann, sitting in London, is a member of the British nation at war. Of course, these talks cannot possibly be regarded by the Tory British officials as diplomatic negotiations, for Dr. Weizmann is their subject and must obey the will of his government, if his loyalty and allegiance mean anything. Obviously then, he cannot tell his government that its closing of the doors of Palestine is internationally illegal. Obviously, then, he cannot negotiate a compromise proposal, such as we have offered, to postpone until after the war all the political and boundary problems of Palestine, thus opening the way for the establishment in Palestine of emergency rescue shelters. When Regent Horthy has announced that every Hebrew who can go to Palestine will be permitted to leave, he cannot criticize, as we must, his Tory Colonial Office's stubborn refusal to establish emergency rescue shelters in Palestine. He cannot say, as we do, that this is a crime second only to Hungary's active participation with Germany in the mass murder of the Hebrew people.

This amateurish attitude symbolizes the present condition of so-called Jewish leadership which is largely responsible for our inability to cope with the catastrophe that has befallen us.

Let us think for one moment of Palestine as an independent state. Who is going to be its political spokesman in

Washington – an American Rabbi? I say, ladies and gentlemen, that once Palestine is an independent nation it will have its own sons represent it and speak for it in the capitals of the world: and I say that in the desperate position of the Hebrew Nation today, we need this representation by our own selves and for ourselves a thousand times more urgently. It is Luxembourgers who represent Luxembourg in Washington; it is Poles who represent Poland; it is Norwegians who represent Norway; it must be Hebrews who represent the Hebrew Nation. Only then the Hebrew people of Europe and Palestine, speaking for themselves, will be in a position to negotiate political and international questions with American, British, and other statesmen.

Today we are still "*schutzjuden*," Jews protected by Americans and Englishmen who are kind enough to "intervene" on our behalf and pay courteous handshaking visits to the foreign secretaries of their own nations.

I am not a politician, and I have no aspirations to public life. I am a Hebrew who, shocked by the plight of his nation, is serving his people to the best of his ability, ever since he looked upon their misery in the ghettoes and slums of Warsaw, Vienna and Budapest. I plead for understanding of the desperate position in which we find ourselves. I plead this understanding from all

Americans, but more particularly from Americans of Hebrew descent – American Jews – all of whom I know are overwhelmed and grieved, despite their own remote and happy lives, by the tragedy that has befallen us – their kin.

These have not been words of criticism that I have spoken tonight. It is not a program of criticism that we advocate. It is a constructive, positive plan that we advance. Yet the leaders of the American-Jewish community, men who have conscientiously and in good faith devoted themselves for many years to the service of the Jewish people both in this country and abroad, are still blindly opposed to what we propose. And this is intolerable. Because the alternative is the *status quo* and *status quo* means additional thousands daily added to the gruesome total of our three million dead.

With the creation of the Hebrew Committee of National Liberation and the announcement of its program, the shapeless mass of Hitler's Jewish victims has become a national entity for which things can be done by the United Nations – and not just by Hitler. If the United Nations really want to save us, and I believe that they do, they must realize that this cannot be done by sporadic expressions of pity and by mere verbal condemnation of what the enemy is doing to us.

What must be done, first of all, is to recognize us as human beings. It is as simple as all that. We, some four to five million Hebrews, are the only people in the world today who belong nowhere. We are not United Nations, and we certainly are not Axis. We are nobodies – we are just not there. If the United Nations are, as Mr. Eden claims, powerless to save our lives, what prevents them from saving our dignity and our honor? As a matter of fact, what drives them to *continue depriving us* of our dignity and our honor? It is strange to see Mr. Eden continuing to hide behind Hitler's shoulders. Even the cynicism of statesmen must have some limitations, particularly at a time when the cream of their countries' youth is dying for noble ideals of freedom and equality, which are piously chanted in the Atlantic Charter and the Four Freedoms.

Once we are recognized as a nation – for all dignified human beings belong to some nation – then the way to the rescue of the surviving Hebrews of Europe will be clear and the action swift. Recognition will set into motion a whole machinery without which the gigantic task of saving four million human beings from a fiendish enemy cannot be accomplished; without recognition, the machinery will not function.

When we are known to the entire world, and to our Godless enemies as a co-belligerent, a member of the United Nations;

When our soldiers, under our flag, are fighting the enemy, and taking prisoners;

When our representatives sit on the Inter-Allied Commission on War Crimes;

When Switzerland, for example, or any other neutral country, becomes our "Protective Power," safeguarding the rights of our nationals;

When Hebrew diplomatic emissaries can negotiate with Turkey, Sweden and other neutrals for cooperation and rescue – for that matter, when Hebrew representatives can negotiate with the United States, Great Britain, and the Soviet government;

Then, and only then, will the *status quo* be broken. A new spirit will set in – a spirit which will make extermination impractical and impossible. For Germany and, certainly, the puppet governments of Hungary and Rumania, cannot afford to proceed with the slaughter of a member of the United Nations, at a time when a United Nations victory is inevitable.

It is because of our infinite admiration for and belief in America that we came to these shores and established on its territory, in exile, a modest beginning toward the rehabilitation of our long-suffering and tormented people.

Our program, which I have outlined tonight, could begin to be effectuated immediately. Only the will is needed – the will of the United Nations.

We have infinite belief in the greatness of the nation whose traditions and whose own struggle for liberation and freedom are the beacon and the hope for the World of Tomorrow – a people to whom we candidly appeal for understanding and help; and with the help of the people of this land we know that the government will listen and act.

ENDNOTES TO CHAPTER EIGHT

1. Noah Lucas, The Modern History of Israel (London: Weidenfeld and Nicolson, 1975, p. 188.
2. Hava Wagman Eshkoli, "The Attitude of the Jewish Leadership in Palestine to the Rescue of European Jewry" (Hebrew); M.A. Thesis, Bar Ilan University, Israel (1976); "Abstract," pp. 1-7.
3. Aaron Berman, "Abba Hillel Silver, Zionism and the Rescue of European Jews": Master's Essay; Columbia University, New York, 1976, p. 26.
4. David H. Shapiro, "The Role of the Emergency Committee for Zionist Affairs as the Political Arm of American Zionism 1938-1944" (Hebrew); PhD. Dissertation, Hebrew University, Israel (1979); Vol. II, p. 349.
5. Yehuda Bauer, American Jewry and the Holocaust: The American Jewish Joint Distribution Committee, 1939-1945 (Detroit: Wayne State University Press, 1981), p. 403.
6. Max Gottschalk to Joseph Hyman, July 28, 1943, File: Organizations, Emergency Committee to Save the Jewish People of Europe 1943-1945: American Joint Distribution Committee Archives, NYC.
7. Minutes, Rescue Committee Sessions Held August 31-September 2, 1943; *I-67 Box 3, pp.

105-106; American Jewish Historical Society Archives, Brandeis University.
8. a) <u>Ibid.</u>, pp. 23-239.
b) Minutes, American Jewish Conference General Committee Session, September 2, 1943; *I-67 Box 1, p. 602; American Jewish Historical Society Archives, Brandeis University.
9. Meyer Weisgal, (N.Y.) to Chaim Weizmann (London), August 11, 1943; Weizmann Institute Archives, Israel.
10. a) Meyer Weisgal, Confidential: Strictly for Zionist Consumption Only, Memorandum on the American Jewish Conference (undated); File: American Jewish Conference Box I; Zionist Archives, NYC.
b) According to a letter sent by Wise to Easterman) British Section of the World Jewish Congress), it was the Zionist leadership in the United States that pushed Monsky to announce the establishment of the Conference. (Wise to Easterman, January 25, 1943, U-142/19; World Jewish Conference Archives, New York City.)
11. Nahum Goldmann to Eliezer Kaplan, January 28, 1943, Minutes of the Jewish Agency Executive, March 21, 1943; Central Zionist Archives, Israel.
12. Meyer Weisgal (N.Y.) to Chaim Weizmann (London), September 3, 1943; Weizmann Institute Archives, Israel.
13. Minutes, General Committee of American Jewish Conference Session Held August 29- September 2, Waldorf Astoria Hotel, New York City, 1943; *I-67 Box 1, p. 599; American Jewish Historical Society Archives, Brandeis University.
14. <u>American Jewish Conference Report of the Interim Committee and the Commission on</u>

Rescue, Commission on Palestine, Commission on Post-War (November 1, 1944), p. 13.
15. Rav Tzair, "Va-ad Artzot HaB'rit" (Hebrew) in Bitzaron, Vol.IX, No.I (48), October 1943, pp. 2-13.
16. Minutes, Administrative Committee Meeting of the American Jewish Congress, June 23, 1944; *I-77 Box 3, p. 152; American Jewish Historical Society Archives, Brandeis University.
17. Ibid., p. 156.
18. Meyer Weisgal (N.Y.) to Chaim Weizmann (London), September 3, 1943; Weizmann Institute Archives, Israel.
19. A. Lourie (N.Y.) to Dr. A. Louterback (Jerusalem), May 6, 1943; S44/250; Central Zionist Archives, Israel.
20. Minutes, American Emergency Committee for Zionist Affairs, May 3, 1943; Zionist Archives, New York City.
21. Wise to Weizmann, July 23, 1943; Weizmann Institute Archives, Israel.
22. Minutes of the Jewish Agency Executive, Report by Berl Locker, October 4, 1943; Central Zionist Archives, Israel.
23. Richard Lichtheim to Nahum Goldmann, dated September 9, 1942, received October 14, 1942, Confidential, Unsorted material; Zionist Archives, New York City.
24. Minutes, Meeting of American Emergency Committee for Zionist Affairs, December 8, 1942; Weizmann Institute Archives, Israel.
25. a) Notes, "Off the Record" Meeting with FDR, the White House, Washington, DC, June 11, 1943; Weizmann Institute Archives, Israel.
b) "Conversation with President Roosevelt, June 12, 1943; Weizmann Institute Archives, Israel.

(Please note: It appears that both documents were written by Weizmann himself.)

26. Minutes, American Jewish Conference Rescue Committee Session, August 31, 1943; *I-67 Box 3, p. 93; American Jewish Historical Society Archives, Brandeis University.

27. Minutes, Discussion between Secretary of State Cordell Hull and Leaders of the American Jewish Conference, September 18, 1943; Weizmann Institute Archives, Israel.

28. Rabbi Dr. Isaac Lewin, "Indeed Your Blood, of Your Souls, I Shall Seek" (Hebrew) in HaPardes, 17:9 (December 1943), pp. 31-32.

29. Minutes, ZOA Administrative Council, April 16, 1944, Box XV; Zionist Archives, New York city.

30. Report to the Jewish Agency leadership by Nahum Goldmann, Protocols of the Jewish Agency Executive, September 29, 1944; Central Zionist Archives, Israel.

31. Tom Segev, "HaYishuv V'Ha Shoah" (Hebrew) in Ha'aretz Weekly Magazine (August 24, 1979), p. 15.

32. Joseph Hyman to Clarence E. Pickett, July 12, 1943; File: Organizations, Emergency Committee to Save the Jewish People of Europe 1943-1945; American Joint Distribution Committee Archives, New York City.

33. Annotated Minutes of Discussion between Abba Hillel Silver and Peter H. Bergson, written (apparently) by Silver, October 12, 1943; Weizmann Institute Archives, Israel.

34. U.S. congress, House of Representatives, Committee on International Relations, Selected Executive Session Hearings of the Committee 1943-1950, Problems of World War II and Its Aftermath – The Palestine Question, Problems of

Postwar Europe, Part II (Washington: U.S. Government Printing Office, 1976), pp. 105, 111, 114.
35. Ibid., p. 231.
36. Summary of Proceedings, Conference of Local Emergency Committee Chairmen Held at Hotel Cleveland, Ohio, December 11-12, 1943; Unsorted material: Zionist Archives, New York City.
37. a) Hadoar, February 4, 1944.
b) Minutes of the Executive Committee of the American Jewish Conference, March 21 1944, *I-67 Box 6; American Jewish Historical Society Archives, Brandeis University.
c) Digest of Minutes of the Interim Committee [American Jewish Conference], November 23, 1943, Box III, American Jewish Conference; Zionist Archives, New York City.
38. Foreign Nationality Groups in the United States, June 6, 1944, OSS Papers, 191 (Declassified 30 October 1979).
39. Leon Kubowitzki, Minutes Administrative Committee Meeting of the American Jewish Congress, June 23, 1944, *I-77 Box 3, p. 66; American Jewish Historical Society Archives, Brandeis University.
40. Minutes, Office committee Meeting, American Emergency Committee for Zionist Affairs, December 11, 1942; Weizmann Institute Archives, Israel.
41. Minutes, Special Meeting of the Committee of the American Jewish Congress and World Jewish Congress, July 16, 1943, *I-77 Box 3, American Jewish Congress; American Jewish Historical Society Archives, Brandeis University.

42. "Draft, Survey on the Rescue Activities of the World Jewish Congress Covering the Period of 1942, 1943, 1944, Submitted to the War Emergency Conference of the World Jewish Congress, Atlantic City, November 13-18, 1944, by the Rescue Department of the World Jewish Congress" (pamphlet), Unsorted material; Zionist Archives, New York City.
43. Kubowitzki, June 23, 1944.
44. Tom Segev

ABOUT THE AUTHOR

Eliyho Matz was born in Tel Aviv in 1948 during the Israeli War of Independence. His parents initially came to Israel aboard the ill-fated ship *Exodus*. His father passed on a love of reading to his young son with the gift of Nikos Kazantzakis' *Freedom or Death*, forever influencing his life.

During the 1967 War, Matz served in the Israeli Paratrooper Brigade. That experience (along with later travel on NYC subways) prepared him to work with two very resolute individuals -- historian David S. Wyman and freedom-fighter Peter H. Bergson, men whose legacies formed the basis for forty-five years of research that led to this book.

Made in the USA
Middletown, DE
30 April 2025